## What Others Are Saying About the South East Asia Prayer Center, and *A Faith to Die For...*

*A Faith to Die For* is a must-read for everyone with a passion for God. Mark's life exemplifies what awesome things God can do when one invests in a life of prayer for the nations. SEAPC [South East Asia Prayer Center], under Mark's leadership, has seen many unreached peoples discipled and transformed by the love of God.

—*Steve Chang*
International Sales Director, W. L. Gore & Associates, Inc.

Mark Geppert is a man used by God to reach His called-out children wherever he is walking and praying. The story of *A Faith to Die For* is a passionate look at how he has become a fearless follower of God.

—*Everett Foss*
Retired Borough Manager of Eau Claire, Wisconsin

Mark Geppert is a humble servant, spreading the good news of Jesus Christ. His commitment to this has shaped SEAPC into a global ministry, focused on spreading the good news to the unreached people of the world in prayer and love. *A Faith to Die For* is an example of the power of prayer and trust in God in a real world setting, which should encourage and empower all who read this work.

—*Ralph Polehonki*
Engineering Director, Ingersoll Rand
Charlotte, North Carolina

Having partnered with this dear brother overseas, I can truly say he was born to be a leader and a visionary. His incredible faithfulness, courage, and service have continued to inspire me in my career and my walk.

—*Dr. David Peng*
Pediatric Cardiologist, Stanford Children's Hospital
Palo Alto, California

In my close association with Mark over the last twenty-five-plus years, he has been a most dedicated, faithful, Spirit-led servant, with the steadfast mission of winning the lost to Christ. While developing and launching the extensive outreach of SEAPC worldwide, his love for the lost has never wavered. This is a man of great integrity, endurance, and deep-abiding faith in his Lord and Savior, all of which sustains his being a powerful writer, speaker, and teacher of the Word.

—*Ken Martin Sr.*
New York Life Insurance Company

Pastor Mark has been walking and praying for God's kingdom to come upon nations. Many nations have been transformed, and some are transforming and preparing to welcome the King of Kings!

—*Pastor Hing-Chai Cheng*
River of Life Christian Church
Santa Clara, California

I have known Mark for over twenty years as a man of great faith and character who has walked his talk. From the start of SEAPC, God has had His hand on it and has blessed it because of Mark's faithfulness. I know that Mark's life is reflected in the pages of *A Faith to Die For*. I hope that all who read it will enter into the greatest relationship a man could have.

—*Gary Lavelle*
Retired Major League Baseball Pitcher

# A Faith to Die For

## Believing God in the Face of Armed and Angry Mobs

# A Faith to Die For

### Believing God in the Face of Armed and Angry Mobs

# MARK GEPPERT

WHITAKER
HOUSE

# A FAITH TO DIE FOR:
## Believing God in the Face of Armed and Angry Mobs

Mark Geppert
South East Asia Prayer Center
P.O. Box 127
Oakmont, PA 15139

ISBN: 978-1-60374-891-9
eBook ISBN: 978-1-60374-892-6
Printed in the United States of America
© 2013 by Mark Geppert

Whitaker House
1030 Hunt Valley Circle
New Kensington, PA 15068
www.whitakerhouse.com

Library of Congress Cataloging-in-Publication Data (pending)

1  2  3  4  5  6  7  8  9  10  11  ᵁᴶ  20  19  18  17  16  15  14  13

*To Noonan*

# CONTENTS

**Part IV: *"I send you...."***

**Part V: *"Do not fear those who kill the body but cannot kill the soul."***

# PSALM 56

### Prayer for Relief from Tormenters

Be merciful to me, O God, for man would swallow me up; fighting all day he oppresses me. My enemies would hound me all day, for there are many who fight against me, O Most High. Whenever I am afraid, I will trust in You. In God (I will praise His word), in God I have put my trust; I will not fear. What can flesh do to me? All day they twist my words; all their thoughts are against me for evil. They gather together, they hide, they mark my steps, when they lie in wait for my life. Shall they escape by iniquity? In anger cast down the peoples, O God! You number my wanderings; put my tears into Your bottle; are they not in Your book? When I cry out to You, then my enemies will turn back; this I know, because God is for me. In God (I will praise His word), in the LORD (I will praise His word), in God I have put my trust; I will not be afraid. What can man do to me? Vows made to You are binding upon me, O God; I will render praises to You, for You have delivered my soul from death. Have You not kept my feet from falling, that I may walk before God in the light of the living?

# FOREWORD

Many have asked the question in more reflective moments, "What can one man do to change the world?"

If you have any doubt that one man, through radical obedience to the lordship of Jesus Christ, can change the world, you need to read *A Faith to Die For*, by my friend and partner in ministry for twenty years, Mark Geppert.

This book reads almost like a Robert Ludlum spy novel; but, in this case, the characters are real and the events actually happened.

You may wonder how one man with very little resources, often with nothing more than a plane ticket and a passport, can travel to some of the most remote and exotic places in the world, only to see God open incredible doors of opportunity every step along the way. The reason is that Mark has one simple principle upon which he has built his life, and that is that *you can trust Jesus to fulfill His Word in your life.*

And though there won't be many of us that will be called to the exotic destinations or life-threatening situations that Mark finds himself in, we all face the challenges of living an obedient life wherever God has placed us in the world.

That's the value of this book, *A Faith to Die For*. It reminds us that God is with us, revealing His power and grace through us to a world that needs us, even if they don't know it!

As I read Mark's book, I appreciated the insight it provided for me in an age when topics of culture and religion appear increasingly on the news. By helping us understand the heart and mind-set of those of other faiths and cultures, Mark helps us all to believe that God can use us in the most extreme circumstances that we face, even if that involves interactions with the neighbor next door, a fellow student, a coworker, or a national statesman.

Read this book and find that God is intimately involved in your daily journey, and begin to expect that the mundane can become the miraculous—a daily journey can become a lifelong adventure—because that's the testimony of Mark Geppert...and the purpose of God for each one of us.

There will be moments when we wonder what we might do next; when we question whether or not there really is an answer to our predicament; when we fear that hope may be gone. It is then that we will discover, as Mark does on many occasions, that we serve a God who never leaves us or forsakes us. (See Hebrews 13:5.)

What can one man do to change the world? As the hymn writer put it, "Trust and obey, for there's no other way," or, in the words of Jesus, "*In this world you will have trouble. But take heart! I have overcome the world*" (John 16:33 NIV). In this book, you will learn how you can "*take heart*," because, yes, you *can* change the world!

—*Dr. Jay Passavant*
Senior Pastor, North Way Christian Community
Wexford, Pennsylvania

# PREFACE

I n hamlets and cities around the world, a drama is unfolding. At first, we see it from a distance, and then up close and personal. Leaders tell us that it is not an "ideological struggle." They insist that militant militias are not driven by religion. In the jargon of globalization, *Arab* has replaced *Muslim* and *local* has replaced *Christian*.

But where does the Christian fit in the new millennium? Is there a place for the faith that has carried billions forward for twenty centuries?

This book was written in Lhasa, Tibet. I had to wait for two weeks for the government of the Tibet Autonomous Region and the People's Republic of China to sign the three-year extension of our contract for the Survey and Treatment of Congenital Heart Disease. This made me a captive in a situation I could not control. I put the time to good use, though; I wrote.

This is a true story of a capture, interrogation, and blacklisting by a nation I dearly love. At present, I cannot return to Indonesia. The most recent attempt to return failed and brought the explanation, "If you come, they will kill you. We cannot protect you, and we do not need a dead American in the streets of Jakarta."

I have been advised on the dangers that await me if this story is told in full, so I have changed a few names along the way. But, the way I see it, there is already a fatwa extended against Christian Americans, so any further threat is redundant.

Having said that, it is my hope that by reading this book, you will grow in faith. Many people today are looking for hope, belief, action, purpose, and a faith for which they can give their lives. Some live selfishly, fulfilling their own desires until they die. Others go to the extreme of adopting a monastic lifestyle, hoping to serve others at the expense of all personal comforts. Between these extremes lies the bulk of the world's population. The majority of people want to know their place and purpose. They follow those who purport to have found a way of hope. They are influenced to adopt faith or cynicism as their overtures become symphonies and the melody is revealed and repeated.

As with many testimony books, you may wonder how the following information could all be the experience of one person. I have to say, looking back, that Jesus has brought me on an amazing journey that started one July morning when He said to me, "I am calling you to preach My gospel to the nations."

I thank God for providing me with a wonderful wife and partner for the journey and two great sons who are serving Him today. I also want to thank our faithful friends with whom we have shared these adventures, as well as the churches and individuals who have paid the way. We are a team and believe we have a voice in this time in which we live.

Sometimes that voice has not been well-received. But, for the most part, I have to say that the multitude is still hungry to hear a message that gives purpose to life. They are waiting in those hamlets and cities to receive the hope that will not fail. They are waiting to hear the Name in which we have hope, not only for this life, but also for the life to come.

God has a Son. His name is Jesus. He died for you, and He is coming back to take you to the wonderful place He has prepared for you.

This is the message, and we are His messengers in the earth.

—*Mark Geppert*

# PART I:

*"Multitudes, multitudes in the valley of decision!"*
—Joel 3:14

*Then Jesus went about all the cities and villages, teaching in their synagogues, preaching the gospel of the kingdom, and healing every sickness and every disease among the people. But when He saw the multitudes, He was moved with compassion for them, because they were weary and scattered, like sheep having no shepherd. Then He said to His disciples, "The harvest truly is plentiful, but the laborers are few. Therefore pray the Lord of the harvest to send out laborers into His harvest."*
—Matthew 9:35–38

*When Jesus went out He saw a great multitude; and He was moved with compassion for them, and healed their sick. When it was evening, His disciples came to Him, saying, "This is a deserted place, and the hour is already late. Send the multitudes away, that they may go into the villages and buy themselves food." But Jesus said to them, "They do not need to go away. You give them something to eat." And they said to Him, "We have here only five loaves and two fish." He said, "Bring them here to Me." Then He commanded the multitudes to sit down on the grass. And He took the five loaves and the two fish, and looking up to heaven, He blessed and broke and gave the loaves to the disciples; and the disciples gave to the multitudes. So they all ate and were filled, and they took up twelve baskets full of the fragments that remained. Now those who had eaten were about five thousand men, besides women and children.*
—Matthew 14:14–21

# ONE

# "WHAT DO YOU WANT FROM US?"

W hat do you want from us? Do you want to convert us all? Do you want us to be your slaves forever? What do you want from us?"

If hatred had a face, it would have been his—turban askew, eyes aflame, mouth spewing the red-hot lava of "jihad jargon." Only the steel bars of the jailhouse window kept us from being consumed by this molten fury.

It was a terrible day in paradise. The gentle breezes of the Indian Ocean and Malacca Strait could not quench the fire. If he had been free, this Indonesian imam would gladly have done Allah a favor and killed an American Christian. His rage was the result of a lifetime of being forced to serve ExxonMobil executives and sleep in a one-room wooden coop, while they danced the night away in high fashion. His people had waited hand and foot on elite Dutch and Americans while the Javanese government collected the few crumbs falling from Aceh's tilted table.

Finally, he and the multitude he served had captured three of the oppressors, as well as their Chinese friend. Justice would be served, if only for one torrid afternoon.

*USA Today* reported that it was a group of missionaries who "ran to the police station for help when faced with the mob." The *Jakarta Post* said it was "another unfortunate incident of Muslim/Christian conflict." While most of the world sat at their breakfast tables, turning the pages of these newspapers while sipping their juice and coffee, a group of people in Aceh, North Sumatra, expressed its indignation at the injustice of what had become an international incident. The events that transpired in March 1999 were just the tip of the iceberg, eventually escalating into larger events that would polarize the world.

We had come to the town that morning in our desire to pray for the Indonesian province of Aceh. A day's journey north of the provincial border, the little town of Perlak is the last police post before a stretch of highway feared by police and freedom fighters alike—a location of mass graves. This stretch of land is one that military personnel do not dare to travel during the night. It is the place where seeds of rhetoric grow into large armies of youth that are ready to blow themselves up for militant ideologies. It is a recruiting ground for extremists, a place where boys become men before they can shave, and where families send their young sons to fight holy wars against the infidels.

We arrived on a beautiful, calm, peaceful March morning, and looked forward to reaching Banda Aceh, which had some of the best scuba diving in the world, beyond the checkpoint. Our hired driver felt that he could make our journey more comfortable by stopping to have a bite to eat before going on the road again. He parked in a central area, and we agreed to go to the market and then venture on to the police station so we could register and be on our way, within the hour. We decided to pair off in twos so that we could experience the quiet little town with another person and share what we had found with each other.

A secondary school had dismissed for lunch and Friday prayers, and we found ourselves in the midst of hundreds of teenagers who wanted to practice their English. Happy to oblige, we haltingly entered into conversation about the NBA and other American topics that interested the youth. The young people were the same ages as our sons and daughters. It was fun to learn how they lived, what they thought about, what they studied, and what they thought was funny. It was a real joy to be accepted by these young people.

It was not long before they had noticed the books we had in the car, and we gladly gave a few to them. Finding that these books were written in their mother tongue of Acehnese, they became very interested. Soon, we had handed out five hundred books and ninety cassette tapes to the teenagers. It had taken about forty-five minutes to do so, and the parents started to call the young people, warning them not to be late for prayers.

In these villages, the mosque was central to the people's lives. Although they had the freedom to choose their religion, there was a civic pressure to abide by Muslim traditions. The farther away one lived from the capital, the stronger the civic pressure was. As a result, the children's delay in reporting directly to the mosque after school was not strictly their parents' concern; therefore, with apology, the students moved along quickly. They got to the mosque at about the same time we arrived at the police station.

Our driver met us at the station. He had to show the officers his appropriate licenses because he had worked for a company in another state and had registered his vehicle there. The police officers were professionally cordial and more than a bit interested in the books and tapes we had brought along.

None of us read the language or spoke it, and so we seized upon the officials' offer to translate the message we carried. They found a tape player and started to play our cassettes. We listened together to the Christian message and soon realized that it was the gospel of Luke and the book of the Acts from the Bible. Not illegal in Indonesia, the gospel message did not set off any alarms with the police. They did caution us, however, about the strong Islamic culture in the area and suggested that we use discretion when sharing the material. We assured them that there was no problem, because the young people had already exhausted our supply. After all, we just wanted to pass through this area to the beautiful city several hours ahead.

Then we were invited into the police station so that they could make a record of our papers and call the station to which we were headed, to give them a departure time and an estimated time of arrival. We were shown to a comfortable room in the back left of the police station, where we were offered cool drinks and made comfortable while a clerk recorded our passport and visa information. The Indonesian police were very professional, thorough, and hospitable. Soon, we found out that they were also well-tempered and very loyal to their guests. They made calls to ensure that our travels would be safe. We really enjoyed the good humor of our newfound friends, along with the conversations about basketball, the World Wrestling Federation, and the recent heavyweight title champion.

Then conflict crashed against the windows. "You mother _____! What do you want from us?" Not quite the material from *Conversations in English, Tape 3*. A thrown bottle accompanied the shout, breaking the window and sending shards of glass throughout the room.

The police quickly pushed us into a hallway for cover and began to reprimand the man at the window. We checked each other for glass and, after finding everyone to be all right, took up a safe place in a cell at the end of the hallway. This would be our shelter for the next five hours, the time it took a very unhappy group of Muslims to vent their hatred, anger, and frustration to their fellow Muslims who protected us (a hapless group that was definitely in the wrong place at the wrong time). We were in the midst of a civil war, with roots that ran too deep for any Westerner to fully understand.

In response to our question, "What do they want?" the police officer replied, "You, dead."

⌣

"Multitudes" form when reason can no longer be found. They live in tent cities in the Sudan or gather on hillsides in Palestine. Multitudes lend their force of numbers to any cause. They can be built on a common fear or a common need. They gather in the deserts of Arizona for the annual Burning Man Festival, a celebration of hedonism. They gather on the National Mall in Washington, D.C., for many different causes. They gather at Tiananmen Square or Trafalgar Square or any other square that accommodates them. They march for causes related to the environment; globalization; abortion; political positions; academic freedom; funding for the research and treatment of disease, such as HIV/AIDS; and common needs, like food and clothing.

Many of them are harmless. They wait for trains, escape heavy rains, and attend sporting events. They walk through deserts to find water. They sell their possessions and carry few necessities on their backs to flee conflict. They search for their basic needs.

When a multitude forms, leaders ask, "What do they want?"

Of the multitudes of Cherokee Indians, who began to move west from the Appalachian Mountains, the leaders said, "Do not worry; they will never survive the winter." When multitudes of people were herded onto train cars to be destroyed by fascism, it was said, "They are an inferior race; we are doing the world a favor to eliminate them." When multitudes of people fled Atlanta in the face of Sherman's March to the Sea, it was said, "Do not be afraid; the South shall rise again."

The problem with the multitudes is that they can be directed and affected by a very small group of extremists. Hatred grows in hungry bellies. It spreads its ruinous roots until murder and suicide become viable options to people who are hopelessly bound to the life-sucking system. A multitude, once in motion, is an irrevocable force that meets the government's immovable hand. Once it swells in the streets and gets a taste of forbidden power, it mutates into a mob that is viewed as a mutiny. Mutiny must be dealt with at all costs, so brothers take up arms against brothers; nations stand against nations. Eventually, people begin to kill each other.

What every mass murderer needs to be successful is a multitude that will follow his or her lead. It makes little difference whether these followers are disciplined and in uniform or undisciplined and blowing themselves up. They are a multitude. They want a slice of the pie; a crumb from the table; the freedom to farm; the right to have a child or to receive an education.

The multitude is not mindless, as some are led to think. It bows down to the one it thinks can give it a better life. It commits to the leader who promises change and reform, because it hopes he or she will be different. It wants to believe that its morsel will become a loaf of bread if it pays the price. And when it begins to appear that it has been used, again, it begins to hope for a better future for its children.

⌒

Would Aceh Province of North Sumatra, Indonesia, be any better if it were governed by Islamic law? Would the rice grow taller? Would the fish return to the Straits of Malacca in abundance, as they did in times past? Would passages to the Straits be free of pirates? Would the profit of ExxonMobil be shared with every home? This multitude, fueled by the rhetoric of a young man instructed in Arabia and armed by money from a man found in a hole in the earth, believes with all its humble heart that the answer is an unequivocal "Yes."

When faced with the first messenger of this multitude, we were frightened to the core. There had been many other multitudes, in other countries, for other causes, but the heat of this fire, in particular, found fodder in our hearts. We could hear the multitude milling about the station. They threw rocks on the roof and bottles at the walls and windows. They chanted and cursed in English and

Indonesian. They broke windows and cried out what they would do to us and to those who protected us.

The euphemistic phrase they used again and again was this: "The situation has escalated." Across from me in the cell was the "Banker," a three-time Golden Gloves boxing champion of the State of New York. With a black belt in several martial arts, and being no stranger to violent situations, he simply smiled. "Stay calm; this is a Level 4. The police will wait until they calm down. Stay away from the windows. Be still. Do not worry; the police know what to do."

I glanced at the "Doctor," a mild-mannered man who was also a close friend of mine. He smiled back. I am sure he was thinking of the other situations we had been through together. But the veins on his forehead looked like they would burst at any moment.

The Asians were calm, poised. They had lived with jihad for decades and knew how to ride out the storm.

I decided to think through past experiences with multitudes. Taking the Banker's advice, I sat down to quietly wait it out.

# TWO

# MULTITUDES ARE HARMLESS

Multitudes are harmless. They gather where there is hope of food, shelter, information, or freedom. As long as no one ignites a fire in them, they just go about their business with no threat of making trouble. But when a firebrand is let loose among them, they turn into a maelstrom of misery. Public security is all about keeping the multitude from hurting itself or others. A "madman" may manipulate the multitude, turning it into a mob of anarchists bent on change at any cost, marching to the beat of its malfeasant melody.

One biblical description of a multitude is *"sheep without a shepherd"* (Matthew 9:36 NIV; Mark 6:34 NIV). Among them, you find the lame, the blind, and those who are too weak to sustain themselves. Within the multitude, children are born and the elderly die. Moses' multitude moved at the pace of the slowest member. Most multitudes mill about as Israel did, taking forty years to journey across an area no larger than an average Texas pasture.

When the members of a multitude are united in the basic belief that they were born to their current state and have no way of escaping, they settle down and suffer silently, hoping for a brighter future someday, in another life. "Well," they rationalize, "things could have been worse. I could have been a worm or some other hapless creature."

"Nepal is a Hindu nation," I was told in 1983. At the time, I was under arrest for preaching the gospel. You see, Christianity is a threat to those who control the multitude, for the reason that it's about a Carpenter who was also a King; a Lamb who was also a Lion. In these seeming contradictions is hope, and hope is a dangerous thing. Hope will cause uprisings. The Romans found that Christianity, if it was not contained by force, would turn the world upside down.

Today, the multitudes in Nepal are the focus of another group—the Maoists, members of the Unified Communist Party of Nepal, who are trying to lead the irresistible multitude against the immovable object of their king's supposed divinity. (They must have missed the past fifteen years of China's release of the multitudes.) These multitudes of people, most of whom just want to grow rice in peace, have become the pawns in the hands of those who would like to own the Himalayas.

⌒

At the request of a national Christian leader, we arrived in Nepal in 1983 with a message of hope: Not only could they have a better life, but they could also go to a better place when their lives were over. This was a hope that would give great joy to their families, as they toiled long hours in the rice paddies. We were perceived as "firebrands" to those in control of the multitude, but these same people were also looking for answers to their own hopelessness.

Our days were spent trekking through some of the most beautiful villages on earth. The Indo-Australian Plate, which carries the multitudes of India, has been in conflict for centuries with the Eurasian Plate, which carries the multitudes of Chinese. Their collision has created one of the most majestic mountain ranges on the planet—the Himalayas.

There, among the upthrusts of time, dwells a humble, hardworking multitude. Like all multitudes, they want something, however simple: They would like to know who made the mountains, how their world came to be, and who maintains it for them. They think that the king of Nepal might be connected to the gods and that, through him, they might share in that beauty. They believe this because they have never considered anything else.

We came to them with something to be considered, and they were keen to hear about it. The plan had been to trek across those mountains and distribute booklets in each small village. The supply of literature, available in four levels of reading ability, from cartoons to advanced vocabulary, had been prepared in

India and shipped by truck to Kathmandu, the capital of Nepal. We flew there from several nations and, after five days of acclimatization, were ready to travel the paths we would soon call home.

The crates of literature looked daunting to our team of forty people, but the zeal of one of the local men lifted us to new heights of belief. Whether he was trying to prove his point or not, he sent us to a village just outside Kathmandu for a training exercise. We had a crate that weighed more than one hundred kilos, containing thousands of copies of the small booklet entitled *Who Is Jesus?* After parking the vehicle in the center of a village, we unloaded the cargo and prepared to distribute the hope-filled material in an orderly way. Once the crate was opened and the contents declared, the multitude surged, literally knocking us to the ground. They desperately wanted the printed material. Once they heard that it was Christian material, they were even more eager to have it; they could not contain their zeal. They wanted the hope it contained.

Our group members had to stand back-to-back and throw the booklets into the air, while the people snatched up every page. They consumed them. Not one booklet was left on the ground, and not one page was torn. The people were like ants devouring sugar. I was amazed at the force of the multitude. We had not called to them; there had been no advance team to tell them we would come that day. It was mid-afternoon in a sleepy little village when the throng had appeared.

⌣

The multitude itself is harmless; but, when pointed toward hope, it becomes an irresistible force. The multitude in Aceh had been pointed toward a hope of independence from Jakarta, the capital of Indonesia. A message of hope from the inequities of life had been preached to them. These Nepalese had heard of a Book that would bring hope, and they were ready to go to whatever lengths necessary to secure one. They did not plan to convert to a new religion; they simply wanted the hope that this book promised.

Will hope make rice grow taller? Will hope make children healthier? Will hope make people more productive? The statistical answer is yes. Studies by the World Health Organization, the United Nations, and Oxford University confirm that cultures with a sense of hope have a higher standard of living. The post-reform growth in China was the result of giving the Chinese people something to hope for again. The grandeur of their former culture was dashed to pieces by the hopelessness of the Cultural Revolution. Since having their hope restored, they have become one of the top leaders in economic growth across the globe.

⌣

My arrest was prompted by the multitude of schoolchildren who had opened our trekking baskets and taken the booklets they contained. I was amazed at their boldness, but our local guide assured me that it was not considered offensive in their culture to look through someone's bag to see what he was carrying. After lightening our load, the children ran off, giggling with delight at having "received" a book.

Soon, an official who had observed us felt it necessary to invoke "public security," and he invited me to explain myself to the local authorities. He and I had a wonderful discussion about multitudes and the need to keep them under control, so that both their safety and ours could be insured. It made perfect sense to me, and I assured him that I would do nothing to cause unrest.

Then, the most amazing thing happened. He asked for a copy of the book. Was he joining the multitude? He had food. He had shelter. He had clothing. He had position. He had authority. He had education. He had a following. What did he lack that would cause him to join the multitude?

He did not have the information his people had received. So, he would not be able to provide public security for them, because they would be living at a higher level of understanding than his own. His only hope to continue serving was to attain the same information they had received, and so he'd had to arrest me in order to obtain a copy of the Book that was filled with hope. He wanted hope, just as they did. You see, he was not all that different from the multitude. In fact, he was one of them.

⌣

That day, I learned to see all men as members of the multitude. We find members of the multitude of humanity in many different places. Some are in the *"valley of decision"* (Joel 3:14). How many people today are in the valley of decision, having yet to reach a decision? Only those who are comatose cannot make a decision. And we don't know for sure how many decisions they will make until they are revived.

The multitudes that must make a decision will follow the same path. They will gather as much information as possible. They will wait as long as they can.

They will do research and interview those who have already made the decision, and evaluate the outcome. They will search their own hearts and read books of wisdom. And then, when the situation allows no more delay, they decide which path to take. And they hope that they are making the right decision.

Winston Churchill once said, "There is no worse mistake in public leadership than to hold out false hopes soon to be swept away."

When American and Great Britain decided to go to war against terrorism, and chose the Iraq as the battleground, they gathered as much information as they could, waited as long as they could, sought information from history and other books, prayed, consulted with the multitudes under the tyranny of terror, and said, "Okay, we will take this course of action; send the troops." And from the day they decided to make a strike against the cousins of Aceh, they hoped they had made the right decision. The justification for war has been, "To give hope to those who were under the tyrannical rule of Saddam Hussein."

Multitudes on both sides of every conflict are looking for hope. They are harmless until someone points their frustrated, futile feelings toward hope. In search of it, they will sail across seas, walk through deserts, chase mirages, deny themselves, and pay whatever price they must in order to achieve it.

⌒

The people who surrounded us in Nepal wanted a book that would give them hope. Because it had been carried to them by Westerners, who seemed to be hopeful people, they were willing give it a try. These same villagers hide from the Maoists and have to be conscripted to military service, because they see the Maoist cause as hopeless. If the king is in contact with the gods, then you have no hope of overthrowing him, even if you kill him and his family. And why should anyone be followed if he fails to offer hope?

The multitude welcomed the Carpenter King to the city because they thought He would overthrow the Romans and they would get back their tax money. But He did not do as expected. Instead, the Romans captured Him, spent a night beating and terrorizing him, and then crucified Him publicly, so that they could bring the multitude back into proper order—for their own safety.

However, that Lamb became the Lion when He rose from the dead, and history records that within two months, the multitude of His followers grew from five thousand to more than ten thousand—and it continues to grow today. The strategy to control the multitude failed because the multitude had found a cure for their hopelessness in the One the grave could not contain.

The multitude is looking for hope. Whether they gather in stadiums or in public lands, whether they walk across parched deserts or sail across shark-infested waters, they search for hope. They want to believe that their leaders are telling them the truth, and they are willing to die to provide hope to their children.

When I was arrested in Nepal, the penalty for changing religions was one year in jail. The penalty for converting someone else to a different religion was three years in jail. The penalty for identifying oneself as a Christian through water baptism was six years in jail. But the multitude was willing to take the risk. Why? Because it had heard about the hope the Christian faith offered and was willing to give all to have it.

The police went through the village to collect the materials. Out of one hundred kilos of booklets and thousands of sheets of paper, only five booklets were gathered as evidence. Even the man in charge of the search did not surrender his copy as evidence. Instead, he quietly slipped it inside his jacket pocket; it was a piece of hope that looked for a better day.

⌒

While the multitude of militant Muslims circled our Public Security sanctuary, I thought about the power of the printed page to propel the multitude into hope. Hope will never make you ashamed. Hope will carry you through death. Suddenly, I realized that all of this thinking about hope was becoming an anchor for my emotions. Looking at the others in our group, I saw the same hope in their eyes. There was no fear, just a certain expectation that the One who had led us to that place would be the One who would take us through it—to this life or to another.

The multitude grew impatient and tried to rush the proceedings, only to be driven back by a volley of rubber bullets and clouds of tear gas. Their impatience told us that the false hope given to them by the "irate imam" was beginning to wear off. They needed another dose of rhetoric before they would rush the building once more. The waiting period gave me time to reflect on another multitude I had seen.

# THREE

## THE HUMAN SEA LAY STILL BEFORE US

The morning sunlight and the gentle breeze created swells that would soon become waves large enough to sweep away any inattentive tourist. Multitudes of men and women sought moments of serenity on the rocky shore that was the Beijing train platform.

The smell of unwashed human flesh melded with the city stench, as if to say, "Just another day of overpopulation." The conductors drove the people away from the steam engines, the coal burners, the officers that demanded identification, and the fifty seats that held two hundred people, as well as the hopes and dreams of being reunited with long-lost loved ones. Thus was China before the reforms—multitudes of people desperately seeking hope.

~

At one time, China was the most advanced nation on earth, until five thousand years of written history were replaced by simple characters and illiterate masses. The hope that had built the Great Wall and the Grand Canal were replaced by communist corruption, which made the Confucian code little more than a pile of stones kept in Xian, along with all the other relics of a long-lost past.

That morning, we were observing a multitude in misery. It was 1985, one of the years tucked into the confusion of the post-Mao era. It had been nine years since the death of the "great hope" of the people—nine years of hopelessness created by the dilemma of deciding whether to give him face or say he was wrong. Every position of leadership was occupied by someone who had marched with Mao. The people wore the blue tunics and trousers of peasants, while the leaders tried to fit their extended bellies into the military's green suits. Of the nation's one billion people, one in five was, in some way or another, connected to those who were in charge of "public security."

Hope had been broken and reduced to one common remark: "I hope the cadre decides to feed us today." Work units traveled in sweatboxes of train cars or marched from task to task. Human value was of no concern anymore. The mindless multitudes of the Cultural Revolution had settled the matter of hope twenty years before, when their parents, then children, had witnessed the consequences of expressing hope. Any individual expression that might give the people a reason to hope was strictly forbidden. Anyone who advanced freedom of thought was considered counterrevolutionary and would meet death before hope could be engendered.

Hundreds of dramas were born depicting Mao as a god—the great deliverer of the masses. The Book of Hope was burned in great rallies, and anyone who was found in possession of a Bible was beaten and imprisoned. In its place were the jumbled verses of the Great Chairman, the Liberator of the Masses. His "Little Red Book" became the standard for thought; and, small as it was, so was its content.

Hope, launched like a Ping-Pong ball from a Chinese paddle, created a rhythmic hope of return, of victory, of individual triumph over challenge, and of the honor of a name rather than a number. When the US and China—the two great powers—joined together, their union was the bouncing Ping-Pong ball that paved the way to our presence at the Beijing Central Train Station, standing on the worn cobblestones. Time had slowly claimed each of the hopeless neo-mandarin magnates, and it was the dawning of a new day in China.

Hope produces patience. We will wait for what we hope for. Just three miles from where we stood, a younger political leader who had not been in the Long March faced the morning with hope in his heart. He saw a new China. He saw a productive people released from unproductive state-run dungeons of despair to live a hopeful life of ownership and enterprise. He held in his heart the hope that China would one day lead the world. He saw a people who no longer slept in the filth of the street, guarded by green suits on the soil of their own land. Hope kept him alive while the system wound down to a handful of people who made the Long March.

Deng Xiao Ping would bring hope to the multitude one day. He would bring the reforms that were so essential—reforms that would insure a future for the people's children and their children's children. Music would be heard from their parks and playgrounds, and people from all nations would gather there for great banquets. They would be allowed to explore space and conduct medical research. The Ping-Pong ball would turn into a basketball, and one day they would host the Olympic Games, bringing all nations together to see what Mao could not see: a China for the Chinese people.

Between Ping's home and the train station is the tomb of Chairman Mao, known as the Mao Mausoleum, in the middle of Tiananmen Square. The blood of one had seized the multitude in the grip of false hope. A system from France known as Western philosophy had swept toward the sunrise in post-war Europe and Asia. A great alliance of false hope had marched multitudes into unproductive bondage. Lenin had learned. Marx and Engels had left their hope-filled Judaism to find a source of identity, along with the masses. Ho Chi Minh had traveled to France to appeal for the freedom of his people, only to find that he had believed in the same false hope. Europe's reaction to the First World War was to pursue a false dream of equality, without recognizing the love and hope of God. And in the spiritual vacuum left by Marx's philosophies, people started viewing their leaders as divine. That little embalmed body in Tiananmen Square became a god to the multitudes; with Mao's death, all hope was lost.

There would be blood shed on those cobblestones. We could feel the tension as we traveled in 1985. The young people, radiant in the hope of their youth, would not be able to sustain the empty ideology that kept them from education and the arts. They were Chinese. They shared the same blood with their talented ancestors—great engineers and architects, great painters and poets, great philosophers, and the world's first linguists. They could not remain mindless multitudes under the oppression of the minority. That morning, they slept under cardboard on the cobblestones, but a day would come when they would no longer be in bondage; they would be educated and connected to the nations they had heard so much about.

⌣

"Hello."

It was a voice, a recognizable sound spoken softly from among the sea of face-less people. A nation, a whole people, called out in that one voice.

I looked at him. His dark eyes arrested my thoughts, and yet I saw hope in them.

"Hello," I responded. "How are you?"

"Fine, thank you. And you?"

Conversation! We were having a conversation. The sea of humanity became a people, and the people became a person, with a name and a mind and a future and a hope.

The metal taps of the soldiers' issued boots broke up our conversation. The young man buried his face, and I turned to greet five green shirts coming to ensure that public security was maintained. After all, if this fellow got a bit of hope, he might run amok and arouse the multitude, and the wave might just break in the wrong, uncontrollable direction of the Great Hall of the People.

They herded us through the sea of people. Arms and legs moved at the sounds of their boots. We were well-protected from thieves, and from anyone else who may have wanted to meet us. After being herded to the foreigners' waiting area, we sat in overstuffed chairs beneath *Casablanca*-style ceiling fans and pondered the plight of the cobblestone-dwelling crowd. From no window could they be seen. Their voices could not reach through the heavy wooden doors. And they most certainly could not use the toilet or the hot water, which cascaded down from a long-forgotten spigot. I tried to stem the flow, to no avail. It would have required hope of future hand-washings for someone to replace the corroded stop-cock. I suppose that, under Mao, they learned that the supply of hot water would never end for the privileged.

Placed in the watchful care of the waiting-room matron, we sipped tepid tea and thought about our journey to Siberia via the Trans-Siberian Railway. We were going to cross Europe to reach London in time to fly back to the States. We had arrived in Tiananmen Square from Hong Kong with a couple of backpacks filled with Bibles. Having distributed them in Beijing, we now had materials for the anti-communists who had ridden the rails in reverse. Herded onto cars, they had left their beautiful cities and winding streams to be reeducated in the mindless wastes of Siberia. With a desire to study art and science, they had been separated from the multitudes.

Stalin once said that he would wipe out Christianity in one generation. These youth had been born to Christian parents in Siberia and were strong in their faith. They hoped that, one day, people would ride the rails and bring them the Book of hope. As we thought about the days to come, we could not help but wonder if we would ever see that young man again.

Sure, he would be the face of the emerging generation around the world. But we wanted to see him personally. Once aboard the train, we decided that we would search every car for him. Statistically, there was a slim chance of us finding him, but hope is not imprisoned by statistics. With hope, we waited for the matron to lead us to the conductor, who would accompany us to our destination and instruct those around us not to "bother [us] with questions or meaningless talk."

The hopeless ones who herd the masses have lost all sense of practicality and reason. Entrapped by their obsession with preventing hope, they naively believe that in a train car with four Westerners, sixty people eager for dialogue are going to ride for three days without saying hello. As soon as the train left the station, the bilingual dictionaries came out. Family photos followed, and we were introduced to a wonderful group of diverse people who hoped to arrive at their destinations with a new contact or friend from outside the mindless mob.

But the comfort of the foreign cabin was not the beach upon which the tide of Chinese humanity rested. That place was, we found, in another section of the train: the rear. Off we went to find our "happy-faced youth."

There are a lot of Chinese people. When you start scanning the crowd for a particular face, it can seem like looking for a needle in a haystack. But each face is unique; no two Asians look exactly alike, and we knew we could find our man if we just looked into the three or four hundred faces on that train.

Once clear of the city, the steam locomotive strained in the aim of reaching the summit of Badaling before plunging into the Mongolian Desert. Chinese people like to smoke and spit. The space between cars is a perfect place for both. It has a breeze, and you can spit all you want and no one will tell you to stop smoking. As the train lurched along at high speed, these couplings provided an adventure in humanity. Passing through the space between cars 17 and 18, I saw our man.

Face washed, hair combed, and travel shirt pressed, he was definitely the one I had seen before. I stood in a space vacated by a smoker/spitter and waited to see if this young man would reach across the great wall of hopelessness to make contact again.

"Good morning." He smiled when he saw I'd recognized the sound of his voice.

My hope fulfilled, I returned the greeting and then released a torrent of high-speed English. His puzzled face put the brakes on my runaway zeal. It is true— hope fulfilled will energize individuals in the multitude to a reckless rampage.

"How are you?" I asked.

"Fine, thank you. How are you?"

We were on *Conversations in English, Tape 1,* for sure.

"What is your name?" I asked.

"Wang Shu Ming," he answered, and then quickly regained the proper side of the conversation. "Where do you come from?"

"America."

The answer brought hope to his eyes.

"Where are you going?" he asked, and I could see the pages turning in the book of his mind.

"I am going to Harbin. Where are you going?"

"I also am going to Harbin." His smile was so broad.

We had made a connection, a similarity, which would be the first stone in a bridge of relationship. The Ping-Pong ball had crossed the net, and we both were experiencing hope.

"Do you live in Harbin?" I asked.

"No." He struggled with the vocabulary necessary for a more complete answer.

We were joined in the passage by four or five others, who leaned close to hear the words. They were curious about English, as well as in who we were and what we were doing. Little did we appreciate the risk he was taking by talking to "foreigners."

"I a student."

It would take years for me to learn that, in Chinese, the verb tense is revealed by the context. He had struggled through a most difficult exercise—trying to remember the verb "to be" and to express it properly. He had given up the struggle and decided to speak as best he could rather than lose the opportunity for brighter things to develop from our exchange.

"These are students also?" I asked, glancing around at the eavesdroppers.

Ignoring my questions, he looked out the smoke-stained window and shuffled his feet. "See you again," he said, then headed back to the section of hard seats designated for those of his rank.

"Okay," I said. Losing hope, I turned to go back to my section, fourteen cars forward. It was then that I saw the green shirt in the window—a reminder that contact with foreigners was discouraged, as it could affect public security.

Coming from a land of free and outspoken individuals, we do not understand the pressures of the multitudes held by hopeless ideology. The youth in Aceh had made contact with us, which posed a threat to those who herded them through life. They would learn Arabic instead of English, guaranteeing that they would never read medicine or pursue other advanced education tracks. However, their ruling class would send their children to Harvard or Oxford or Sydney so that a representative contact could be made with the outside world. Reforms would be very slow in coming to the masses. For many more years in China, any young person who found a way to learn English would be subject to herding by a mindless green shirt whose only task was to keep him moving in the prescribed circuits of life—far enough from the horizon to prevent hope from ever being seen.

That night, he risked it all. We would arrive in Harbin in the morning, and he wanted desperately to have a hope for the future; so, while the green shirts slept, he made his way to the foreigner car. With the stealth of a night cat, he sought me out.

"What is your name?" he asked excitedly.

"My name is Mark," I answered, leaving complete control in his hands.

"Are you a Christian?"

I was shocked at the question.

"Yes," I answered.

"Have you any 'bread'?" He was asking about Bibles.

"Yes," I answered. "I have five 'whole loaves.'"

"May I have them?"

His hope-filled voice touched a fountain of emotion in my heart.

"Of course," I responded. "Here they are."

"Good-bye." It was final, and yet eternal. Two words that have warmed my soul ever since.

How had he known? Had the cobblestone welcome been a chance meeting? Had someone told him we would be on that train? In those days, you never knew who knew you. We had to be so careful with everything. A wrong word could mean jail for many people. Now, with Bibles printed and purchased openly in China, with churches open and every service packed, I often wonder if hope was fulfilled through those young ones who rode the rails.

⌒

My thoughts were interrupted by another crashing bottle and the sound of gunfire. This was a tense situation. I looked at the Banker, and he held up five fingers. Only halfway to ten, the level of crisis, only halfway to a crisis. How long would it be until these young people would know the hope that drove my young Chinese friend to find me on a moving night train? Would they ever find it? Would they ever be free of the hatred and killing? Or would the Irate Imam control their lives forever?

# FOUR

# THE MULTITUDE HAS MANY FACES

The multitude is a mosaic of colors and shapes. No eye in a multitude looks exactly like any other eye. When massed together and motivated in the same direction, they become an irresistible force headed for an immovable object. When I was asked to visit Jakarta, Indonesia, during the student demonstrations leading up to the fall of the Suharto regime, I wondered at the wisdom of a Westerner being anywhere near the place.

Local leaders with whom I had spent days in prayer felt that the young people were becoming pawns in the hands of masters who would use them to raise civil war in their country. It was the end of the school term, and the least that could be said was that their education was going to be interrupted. Remembering our own campus demonstrations, like the four tragic student deaths at Kent State University in 1970, I agreed to meet them in Jakarta.

Indonesia is a beautiful place. Its fifteen thousand islands are magnificent pearls strung through crystal-clear waters, with sandy beaches and majestic volcanoes; it is a sight to behold. From the beginning of time, it has been the habitation of nations speaking their own languages, embracing their own cultures, fashioning their own gods, and preserving their own hopes and dreams.

After the World Wars, someone decided that unity among the peoples was the way to provide a future hope for generations to come. And since the Dutch had colonized the islands in the first place, they were the logical stewards of the riches that would surely develop for the benefit of the multitudes. The only difficulty in that stewardship was that several other groups also claimed the right to give hope. The native population had been there first. Then, about six hundred years ago came the Chinese, who, in a slick cohabitation deal with the natives, decided to stay out of the local government and just make money.

Around the year 1305, the first Muslims came to Aceh and spread quickly throughout the western islands. They, too, were tradesmen. The cultures coexisted quite well, as long as they did not try to unify the languages, education, and currency. Even the Dutch were sensitive to the fact that the ten thousand distinct ethnic groups of Indonesia had no desire to intermarry, unify their economies, or exchange goods.

After the war, with the Japanese gone, control of Indonesia reverted back to the Dutch. The locals were not pleased, and a bloody war ensued, as the people united in a common purpose to rid themselves of their foreign masters. This was not difficult, as the post-war Dutch were not all that strong.

The multitude was unified under the leadership of President Sukarno and the famous teacher Muhammad Hatta as Vice President. The Sukarno-Hatta regime continued along a bumpy path until recently, with the daughter of Sukarno, Mrs. Megawati Sukarno Putri, sitting on the throne over a nation of two hundred million people.

It is now estimated that the nation is 90 percent Muslim, making it the largest Islamic nation on earth. And the multitude continues to look for hope.

The Indonesian political process is best described as "motorized mayhem." The youth—the lifeblood of the multitude—are paid to cavort about the streets, driving motorbikes or riding in truck beds, while declaring their loyalty to the candidates of the various parties. During "Green Week," they all wear the green shirts and chant the green slogans and make a lot of noise about the green candidates. The following week, "Red Week," the same youth don red shirts and chant red slogans and make noise about red candidates. The following week is "Gold Week," and so on.

The major problem with this system is that it tends to undermine any hope of peaceful and sincere elections. Intimidation by mindless mobs is dehumanizing, at best. One day, three young men wearing green headbands and T-shirts drove up on the sidewalk to shout the virtues of their candidate in my face, while revving the motor so loudly, it was impossible to discern anything they were saying. The subliminal message was very clear: "This is our time to feel power and control. It is the only time we have, so we are enjoying it."

People without hope will always grab at the straws intimidation holds out to them. I have often wondered if any of those kids had been recruited and trained for the ultimate power trip—entering "paradise" by doing Allah the favor of killing infidels with the push of a button. They were cute on their bikes with their T-shirts, but they would certainly look different holding a sword over the head of a hapless truck driver who only wanted to feed his family.

"We really need to pray," my friends said. "These elections are different. Mobs have begun burning buildings, pastors are being killed, and we feel that students are going to be dragged into it."

These friends of mine love their country and, as part of the Christian minority, feel their only answer is to pray. They have no interest in ruling. They do not want to take over the leadership; they just do not want the heated rhetoric and false hopes of a political party to ignite fires of hatred that cannot be quenched. Indonesia has released the multitude to determine their own course, and there are people pushing for the removal of anyone who disagrees with their ideology.

For this pre-election trip, we chose a five-star hotel as our "prayer tower." From our window, we could see the formations of soldiers and police sent to defend the national congress building. We took turns praying throughout the night. We were impartial in our devotion, simply asking God to protect this multitude. They were dispersed in their representative colors, and from that pristine perch, they looked for all the world like sheep without a shepherd. With dawn came the stirring of hearts that would bring us to one of the most interesting situations with a multitude I have ever witnessed.

"Last time, they gathered at the Sukarno-Hatta Monument to begin their march," my host offered. "Let's go over there and see if that is the plan today." He checked us out of the hotel, saying that we would be safer spending that night at his home, outside Jakarta. He was torn between our mission and our safety, trying to find within his soul an island big enough to accommodate hope for both.

"Do you think we could stay here another night?" I asked. I was already suffering separation anxiety.

"No, Mark," was his gentle reply. "Friends we have in the government feel that this area could be a war zone by evening. You will come out and stay with us. We do not want to lose you to an angry mob."

*What does he know that I don't?* I wondered as we waited for the driver to bring his car.

The driver dropped us off at the memorial and left to deliver our bags to the place where we would be staying that night. We were joined by some church members, and all of us took time to pray for Indonesia.

The hope that the multitude held in their hearts had provided Indonesia with education and improved human rights. They had created a government that was for the people and by the people. But greed and dreams of wealth had corrupted those ideals. In the eyes of the multitude, their new leaders had become the "New Dutch." They had skimmed 20 percent of the economic profits into their families' pockets. The demonstrations we saw that day were the corporate complaint of a multitude that had believed in a false hope. They would wear different colors, shout different slogans, and carry different placards, but their cry was the same: "You told us to put our hopes in you, but you didn't produce!"

Shifting our location to the main university, we found a sea of students pouring into the streets. No hasty exodus from exams, this was a well-planned public protest against the government. The multitude demanded change. The speeches were well prepared and delivered with finesse. My host was moved to tears many times, and, as a friend, I tried to feel what he was feeling, even though it was not my country. I love Indonesia, but I could not bridge the gap into the depths of his emotion. This giant of a man stood and wept as the future of his nation cried out their hope.

They began to move. Slowly, calmly, linked arm in arm, the students moved through the streets and thoroughfares of Jakarta. Size makes a statement, but self-control makes a declaration. This mob was self-contained. They checked everyone who wished to join them. They wanted to be certain that none of the instruments of violence so common to Indonesian demonstrations of the past was present that day. They were not against anything; they were *for* the future of their nation. I was proud to walk with them and to think of the future that could be realized, if only the interest groups would allow these young people to emerge.

I lost my sense of direction. Usually, if I have walked a city, I am pretty secure in my memory of it. I had become enthralled with the hope of these young people.

After hours of flowing with them, I realized I had no idea where I was. My friend seemed peaceful, but I began to get the sense of some coming difficulty. As we rounded the bend, I saw it.

We had come full circle through the city and were approaching the congress building. The driver appeared, and we separated from the crowd, seeking sanctuary in his car. He took us to a place near the hotel, and we hunkered down. Now, behind the military position, we sought a place for prayer. As we crossed through a parking garage near the congress, we were greeted by companies of soldiers preparing for confrontation. They seemed quite formidable.

"Mark," my friend called to me, "how close do you want to get? This looks pretty serious."

"Let's see how far we can go before they stop us," I responded, knowing the soldiers would defend "public security."

We moved up a walled walkway that deposited us to the right of the car park of the congress. From there, we could walk through the lines of police until we came to the commandos and the marines. About five hundred meters ahead of us were the students. They had stopped in the street and were listening to speeches. We were in the midst of the military deployment on the southbound side of the highway. All traffic had been rerouted to the northbound side, but even those five lanes stood no chance of containing the vehicles.

A new multitude of youth approached from behind our position. They were not the docile student-types. They wore headbands and carried sticks and other home-fashioned weapons. It was not clear if they had come to "help" the police or if they had another agenda. We could feel the squeeze, and we prayed as the captain went over to negotiate with their leadership. Quite vocal and gesticulating wildly to express their dislike of the government and disdain for authority, this multitude threatened to turn an interesting study in democracy into a bloodbath.

"These are the ones you have to watch," my friend said. "Sometimes they are paid by the government to start trouble so that the troops can rush in and 'restore order.' Watch about five rows back and see if they have weapons."

The marine next to us said, "Where do you come from?"

*Wow,* I thought, *polite conversation in the midst of strife. This is a man who knows the situation.*

"I'm from America," I answered. "Have you been there?"

"Yes," he responded. "We were there last year to train with the US Marines."

"Did you enjoy it?" I asked.

"Of course. It is the most powerful country in the world and a very nice place to be."

"Thank you."

I felt better having a friend in the marines. His eyes never left the field in front of us as he spoke.

"Do you understand what is going on here?" he asked. "This is all about power. Today, we have it. The students will have it when they finish school. The gang across the way has no power. They never will, because they do not have the discipline necessary to have power in their lives."

"Thank you for that explanation. What do you think is the source for all power?"

"Well, everyone has to believe in something that will take care of him. You can believe in God, yourself, your captain, or your imam, but you have to believe in something or someone."

I was startled by the matter-of-fact way in which he presented his thoughts. This was not a mindless marine. This young man was about the same age as those in the other groups. I wondered what a good thinker like him was doing out here.

"So, you chose the military route?"

"Yes, sir," he responded. "At the end of the day, the military has the power in our country. When these two groups have had their say, we will still be standing."

Our conversation was interrupted as he came to alert position, bayonet fixed. The group of students had begun to move toward us. The group on our left had stopped behind the highway barrier. It appeared they were beginning to lose hope in their conquest. My new friend was tuned to his commander, and I was in the way. I moved out of the formation and, standing on the side, prayed for all to be safe.

Two multitudes, one in uniform and one in Levis and T-shirts, faced each other over a slowly diminishing space of a five-lane paved highway. The pressure built with each step. Rumor had it that the students would rush the police and military to seize the congress, then make a televised address to the nation.

Evidently they had never talked with this young marine. He was sure it would never happen.

The gap shrunk to a space of two hundred meters. The marines had not lifted a voice or a weapon; they just stood there, an immovable object.

A group of about fifty students came within one hundred meters of the marines and began to sing, chant slogans, and dance. It was an expressive demonstration, but the message was lost on the marines. They were joined by a slight, well-dressed man and woman with a stepladder and a television camera. I was amazed when my host identified the woman as Maria Ressa from CNN. She was going to report live on the demonstration.

She interviewed several members of the group as the rest of them continued singing and waving banners. Then she thanked them and left. It was the most amazing bit of news reporting I had ever seen. I later viewed the report, and you would have thought that every student in Indonesia was dancing one hundred meters from congress.

After Ms. Ressa left, the smaller group assimilated into the larger one, and together they resumed their advance on the marines' position. As they came within 100 meters, the marines came to the full ready, and their officer stepped forward about 20 meters and announced to the students that their demonstration had gone as far as it would be allowed to go.

Two of the students stepped out and shouted some discourteous remarks at him, and then at the multitude behind him. They stood their ground, and the rest of the students started moving forward again.

I called out to my new marine friend, "Want to see some real power?" Then, extending my hands to heaven, I cried, "Lord, make these kids sit down."

They did. They sat right down. I would not have believed it myself, if it were not for the multiple hundreds of military witnesses present. The situation had looked hopeless, but there is always hope in prayer. Those young people sat down in the street, contemplated their future, and then, in the calm declaration of their quality, quietly got up and dispersed.

The multitude has a face. It is made up of many faces. Each one is unique. Even under pressure, the Indonesian is all smiles. The students were smiling. The marines were smiling. The commander was smiling. The situation was a controlled expression of their shared desire for hope.

When an Indonesian stops smiling, the lava of a thousand volcanoes cannot compare to the fury that is about to spill out. Centuries of repression at the hands of foreign invaders and charm-wielding spiritists ignited the timeless passions of these tribal, territorial, and traditional inhabitants of the land. In recent years, some have reverted to cannibalism, as the Dayaks have repelled the Madurese in the conquests of cultures gone mad. The mass graves in Sumatran paradise are filled with Acehnese and Javanese, and into the tropical tapestries of Timor and Ambon are woven the scarlet threads of the blood of their sons.

⌣

Judging from the sounds outside of our cell, no one was smiling. We were about to have a visitor. The multitude was about to have a face. And what a face it would be. Not the Irate Imam; not the youth, so hungry for hope. This would be the face of authority.

# FIVE

# TEN MEN TURNED THE CORNER

Ten men turned the corner and walked toward us. Known to each other, they carried the weight of an escalating situation. The five in uniform moved with the confident strides of men trained for such a circumstance. Those in civilian dress were showing the strain of having thrown back the first organized attack by this group of radicals. I was relieved that the Irate Imam was not with them, for I thought he would get physical if we were brought face-to-face.

The captain of police was the first to speak. He gave us an overview of the situation. We had arrived at the wrong place, at the wrong time, and had done the wrong thing. The Muslim population was upset about the books and tapes, but that was not the main problem. They saw us as intruders into holy territory and felt compelled to cleanse the land. That meant our removal. He had arranged for our car to be allowed to pass through the mob. We were to wait a few minutes and then follow him and the five uniformed officers to the car, get in, and get out of town, headed back to where we had come from, never to return. He had negotiated this solution.

From behind his well-apportioned frame stepped a man about my age. He had pulled an "I Love America" T-shirt over the top of his rotund physique. The effect made the bald eagle appear walleyed. Trying not to laugh at the comic relief before me, I bit the inside of my lower lip and focused on his sweating brow, which was about a foot away from my own.

"You are so stupid!"

I'm not sure which hit me first: the fire of his passion or the spittle that accompanied his insults. Here was a man who had waited a long time to get an American in a compromised situation so he could finally tell him exactly how he felt about things. I wondered how many times an employer, teacher, or boss had said those words to him. The phrase had lain at the bottom of this volcano for a long time.

"What have you done?" he demanded.

He was trying to make a point, but his body was trembling with such passion that his mind was receiving the verbal missiles in an erratic staccato, which flew from his lips in like fashion. His eyes, fixed on mine, were actually trembling in their sockets. The fire of his fury emblazoned his brow, and his veins were like the tentacles of a giant squid, reaching to his temples. I have never seen an angrier man.

"Why have you come here?"

Fury does not want an answer to rapid-fire questions. But, fearing for his health, I answered anyway.

"Sir, I am very sorry for the problem we have caused here. Please forgive us and allow us to go. We will bother you no more."

With a grunt, he closed what little space remained between us. "You are fools. We have peace here. We are one nation. I am a Moslem; this man is a Christian. We are good friends and neighbors. We have known each other since we were small children. Our children are friends. This is not Ambon. We have peace here."

He had used apology-purchased time to put together his entire instruction. He was beginning to calm and had diverted attention to his "friend."

I glanced at his friend. He had the classic look of a person who had been dragged somewhere against his will by someone who had an idea. He no more wanted to be there than we did. A "Christian" in the presence of four other Christians, and he had nothing to say in any language. I looked at him with great love. If he was a Christian, then he would have gained hope from knowing that he was not forgotten by his brothers who lived in real freedom. If he was not a Christian, then his ruse would not go unnoticed in heaven.

I nodded at him, trying to discern some flicker of hope in his eyes. There was none that I could see. His only distinguishing characteristic was the hat he wore—a cap falsely declaring New York the champion of a title.

In a way, Indonesia is the land of the "losers." Before the championship game of every major American sport, T-shirts, ball caps, and other merchandise are printed, proclaiming victory for both sides. Hundreds of thousands of "authentic" merchandise are made to meet the demands of thousands of fans caught up in the frenzy of victory. After the game, when the outcome is sealed, all merchandise declaring the losing team as victors must disappear. Instead of throwing away or destroying the inaccurate merchandise, most professional sports franchises strike a deal with charity organizations that ship it off to Third-World countries—countries like Indonesia. I suppose the argument is that Indonesia is far enough away from America for no one to really know or care which team actually won.

The hat would have fit a person about two-thirds his size. Perched atop his round head, it seemed to say, "I am uncomfortable with this situation and have no idea why I am in this place. They just grabbed me and stuck this stupid hat on my head and told me not to talk. Please do not prolong this, because I want to get out of here."

Seeing the fear in his eyes, I repeated my apology, then looked past the now still volcano to the captain of police.

They took their leave, and we prepared to follow.

"We will come and get you," the captain said. "There is a large crowd outside; they may shout at you and throw things. Please stay with my men and move quickly to get into the car. We will hold them off."

He said something to the Indonesian driver, checked to see that the men in hat and T-shirt had cleared the area, and then led us to the front of the station. We hastened to get into the car, but the mob rushed across the highway, throwing rocks, bottles, and insults, as they tried to capture their American trophies. We retreated back inside the building, but our driver had disappeared, blending into the crowd.

It wasn't long before the smoke told the story. Our car was being burned. Wondering about the things in it, and thankful that our passports were safe in the possession of the police, we reassembled in the cell and reassessed the situation. Strain was on our faces, but calm was in our hearts. We had an assurance that it would all work out.

The captain of police asked us to stay away from the windows. He seemed very upset. As he was speaking to us, the electric power was cut off. He looked at us with consternation, turned on his heel, and took command of the situation. He, too, had become a target of the fury of this multitude.

# PART II:

*"These signs shall follow...."*
—Mark 16:17 (KJV)

*And He said to them, "Go into all the world and preach the gospel to every creature. He who believes and is baptized will be saved; but he who does not believe will be condemned. And these signs will follow those who believe: In My name they will cast out demons; they will speak with new tongues; they will take up serpents; and if they drink anything deadly, it will by no means hurt them; they will lay hands on the sick, and they will recover."*
—Mark 16:15–18

*And with many other words he testified and exhorted them, saying, "Be saved from this perverse generation." Then those who gladly received his word were baptized; and that day about three thousand souls were added to them. And they continued steadfastly in the apostles' doctrine and fellowship, in the breaking of bread, and in prayers. Then fear came upon every soul, and many wonders and signs were done through the apostles. Now all who believed were together, and had all things in common, and sold their possessions and goods, and divided them among all, as anyone had need.*
—Acts 2:40–45

# SIX

# MULTITUDES WANT HOPE

Multitudes want hope. When believers in a cause have hope, they take action. They are all about action. "What do you do?" seems to be their favorite question. They have developed from the idealism of the students sitting on the cobblestones of Jakarta to the action figures who ride bikes through the streets, shouting political slogans. In the mind of the activist, "What do you think?" has become "What do you do?"

The people making headlines these days are radicals who believe in a god who would direct his followers to hijack a plane full of innocent people and fly it into a building full of innocent people, to protest the treatment a highly paid US operative received in a war between Afghanistan and Russia. That may be a bit of an oversimplification, but if enough members of the multitude can be persuaded to believe it, they will become believers; and in airports around the world, innocent travelers will be asked to remove belts and shoes before being allowed to board their flight.

One believer in a cause, totally committed, can change the course of human history.

Ivana Madzur is such a person. In 1985, there was still a wall in Berlin, and the Russians occupied Ivana's native Poland. Our group had crossed Siberia from

China, and we were hungry. We stayed at Szymanski's house, near the Warsaw train station, and decided to take advantage of a beautiful spring morning by touring the Old City of Warsaw. Being a fan of the author Leon Uris, I deeply wanted to see the ghetto from which a band of young Jews believing they could overthrow Hitler had started the Warsaw Uprising.

In the northwest corner of the Old City Square, there is a sewer grate. It probably doesn't mean much to those who pass by, but after reading Uris's *Mila 18*, it had come alive to me. It was through this grate that couriers entered a maze of sewer pipe that carried their preteen bodies to leaders of the resistance. Their courage will never be forgotten. They had stepped out from the multitudes of people who acquiesced to Hitler's maniacal, systematic destruction of their city, their world, and their hope.

To the right, in front of the grate, is a museum dedicated to the underground resistance. I could have spent a year on the second floor alone. Sights and sounds I had tried to imagine while reading by flashlight hidden under blankets, lest my parents enforce their edict "Get to bed," came to life as I stood in that place. A group of youth who decided they would rather die believing than live without hope had left a legacy that inspired their neighbors to organize and resist tyranny to the death, until they were sold out to Stalin.

The smell of pizza made me aware if my hunger, enticing me from my reverie. One member of our team had a medical condition that required he eat every six hours, and he had found a pizza place. We stepped reverently across the grate and entered a wonderful world of sights and sounds like those of the home we had left one month prior. The people looked like Americans. The cheese smelled like America. The tables and chairs felt like America. We overheard the language of America as a young guide shared information with her English charge. The familiar environment and warm food helped us to relax, and we began to laugh about many of the adventures we had faced on the Trans-Siberian Railway. Our team was composed of believers who took Jesus literally when He said, *"Go into all the world and preach the gospel to every creature"* (Mark 16:15).

We were surprised when a young lady approached and asked us if we were Christians. Evidently, we had let down our guard in the familiar surroundings. She invited us to a meeting that night at a Catholic charismatic fellowship outside Warsaw. Intrigued, we agreed to go, and arrangements were made.

That evening, we met with a group of about twenty students. They sang, accompanied by guitar, and raised their hands in praise in charismatic fashion. We shared some stories from our journey and brought a report of the church in China and Mongolia and the contacts we had made in Siberia and Moscow. Subject to the oppression of communist Moscow, these Christians were thrilled to hear of other believers on campuses across the railway. Of particular interest were the fellowships we had found in Irkutsk and Novosibirsk. We spent a wonderful evening with them and afterward returned to the city filled with wonder at the faithfulness of the Lord.

I met and worked with Ivana, the woman from the pizza parlor, many times after that. Through a series of events, I was invited to spend three weeks in Poland, traveling to universities and sharing my faith with students. At one time, I was invited to join a bishop in a public observance of Communion, and I was privileged to meet with many leaders of the Solidarity union movement, which eventually toppled Soviet power there, returning control of Poland to the Poles. But my experiences in that wonderful land paled in comparison to the testimony of this young woman.

Ivana is a believer. Belief activates hope to performance. Signs follow those who believe. Nations are changed by those who believe. Jesus said of those who believe in Him that they would relieve the oppressed, they would bring healing, and they would be able to communicate with many nations. Ivana is such a believer.

It was on my third visit to Poland that a colleague of hers told me the story Ivana was too modest to tell me herself. As a schoolgirl, she had a profound faith in Jesus Christ. She believed with all of her little being that Jesus would keep her safe in the face of whatever oppression came at her. She was never afraid to pray for a friend or give a loving hand when there was a need. She believed in her Bible and carried it in her backpack.

Hers was a poor people in a poor country. All the material goods they produced rode the rails back to Mother Russia. The men and women of their villages worked long hours for little wages; the proceeds were sent to Moscow to fuel the arms race.

The students attended a rural one-room school that was heated by a single coal-burning stove in the center of the room, and the punishment for any joyous behavior was to carry up a load of coal from the coal bin beneath the building.

Ivana was always dressed immaculately in homemade clothing, and it was the delight of the schoolmaster to send her to the bin, knowing that she would be covered with coal dust upon her return. He mocked her every day, trying to defeat the faith so strongly entrenched in her heart.

One bitter winter day, the schoolmaster was found to be in a particularly nasty mood. All the children were on alert to his desire to harm someone. He chose Ivana. Cheeks rosy from the winter wind, she entered the warm school with a cheery greeting and walked right into the hateful wrath of a man mad with hopelessness. After ridiculing her before her classmates, he sent her outside without coat, scarf, or mittens. He issued the edict that no one was to help her; anyone who as much as looked out through the frosted window to check on her condition would join her. It was his intent that the girl should freeze to death.

As this Christian sister shared Ivana's story with me, I pictured the frail pre-teen standing there, shivering, in the wind-driven snow and ice. My heart breaking, I asked her to continue.

They passed the day without any breaks; no one opened the door or peeked out the window. When it was time for dismissal, at 3 p.m., they gathered up Ivana's coat, gloves, and scarf and went out to retrieve her body, sure that it was frozen by now.

Yet there she was, still standing, with hands lifted to heaven, worshipping the Lord. The grass at her feet was green and fresh as spring. Her skin was not cold at all. She was radiant in the power of the Lord. When they called to her and embraced her, she seemed to return from some faraway place. She reported no sense of time passing. She had been kept in the timeless warmth of the One in whom she believed.

All of Ivana's classmates became believers that day. The schoolmaster was transferred, and life went on. But Ivana's story began to travel from school to school. The telling of it put hope in the hearts of students across Poland. By the time I traveled with her, the movement was fifty thousand believers strong, poised to transform campuses across the nation.

After Ivana and I had worked together for the last time, I asked her where she would go next.

"Oh!" she exclaimed. "Some of my school friends have found a flat in East Berlin that faces the wall. We are all going to live there and pray around the clock until that wall comes down. We believe Jesus is going to set us free from the atheists from the east."

Ivana believes in a God who gives life. She had found the God who will sustain the oppressed and set the captive free. As I watched the footage of Ronald Reagan telling Mikhail Gorbachev to tear down the Berlin Wall, I could not help but wonder if God's camera was focused on a group of students gathered in a little room on the east side, calling on Him to do the same thing. Ivana is a believer. She acted upon her beliefs, and she became the deliverer of thousands.

⌣

"*What have you done?*" The question from the man in the T-shirt came back to me.

*What have I done?* I asked deep within my heart. I am a believer; but what have I done to glorify the Lord in whom I believe? Do I follow and obey Him? Am I willing to risk my life to change nations?

My answer was surrounding the building. The sound of gunfire again brought me from the Old City in Warsaw to this small town in Indonesia. I looked around at our group and thought, *Yes, we are believers. We would go the limit for the Lord we love.*

# SEVEN

## BELIEVERS GO OUT AND PROCLAIM A MESSAGE

B elievers create pockets of belief everywhere they go. The followers of Jesus circled the known world within two hundred fifty years of His ascension. The followers of Gautama Buddha also have reached around the world. Islam has taken the book of the Prophet into every nation. Sitting in the cell in the world's largest Muslim nation, I began to think that perhaps the world was getting too small for all of us to walk about with our beliefs. Either we will have to agree to coexist in peace, or we will have to kill each other until no one is left.

I am a believer. I travel to tell the story. I believe enough to act. The thought drove my mind to the furthest reaches of my travels to talk about Jesus.

There is a nerve in your leg that cramps when you look up to see how far you have to climb. It happens on stairs and fire escapes. It happens on treadmills when you realize that only ten minutes have passed. But it really happens when you are trekking in the Himalayas.

We had been walking at a brisk pace up the hill from the gateway of Beni. Central Nepal is the trekking capital of the world, and this trail is traveled by thousands each year. It takes you to the Annapurna Sanctuary, home of the world's most beautiful sunrise. The path winds its way along a stumbling stream from 4,000 to 17,000 feet, an ascent that takes days for most foreigners to complete; the route is dotted with guesthouses situated at eight-hour intervals. We were on our way to the pass at Dharapani and were looking forward to the hot springs found along the way.

I saw him coming down the trail toward us, about ten minutes off. The nerve in my leg cramped, and the breath fled from my lungs. I forced myself to keep climbing, energized by the thought of seeing this man again. He was wearing the Penn State football jersey I had given him, and, with an umbrella slung across his razor-thin shoulders and a scarf flung haphazardly about his neck, he looked for all the world like a movie set escapee.

I altered my pace and took to the middle of the path, waiting for him to see the obstacle. Just as he stepped down to my level, I looked up and smiled gently.

His face filled with surprise and recognition.

"You are a terrible guru!" he exclaimed. "You are terrible. I threw off my old guru for you, and you never came and gave me a word. I waited every day for your return, and you never came."

"I am on my way to you now," I offered lamely, "and you will not be there when I arrive. Such a disappointment you have given me. Where are you going?"

"You told me to make believers of all the children I taught, so I shared with them from the Book, and they all believed. There is no more work for me to do on that mountain, so I am going to the next mountain to tell them the good news. You said you would come, and now, so late, you come to me." Joy filled his eyes as he shared the good report.

"I see you have kept the shirt," I offered.

"Yes, it is the mantle of my guru." He thrust back his shoulders to imitate my size.

"You look great," I said, and sent him on his way, another believer going to great lengths to make other believers.

The first climb I had made to this man's village had been somewhat difficult. In our desire to complete the lower loop of the Annapurna, we had overextended ourselves and were not able to make it to the Dharapani camp. We decided to pitch tent in a schoolyard and exchange some cash and gifts for water and firewood. He had been the teacher, and we had great fun speaking English and telling riddles. Nepalese love riddles.

A large crowd of interested students had gathered to hear our conversation. A typical village teacher, he had become their key to understanding the world outside their high mountain perch. He translated my words for them and theirs for me, and we had a wonderful evening. The students were bright and asked well-informed questions. One was about my traveling companion, Jim, an African-American with curly white hair—quite a contrast with me, a German-American with blue eyes and a big belly.

They wanted to know why Americans come in so many shapes and sizes. They were very keen on trying to rub off Jim's black and my white; and, to our delight, we found that they felt related to him but foreign to me. How wonderful it was to have them peer deeply into our eyes and try to pull the hair from our legs. There is at least one place on earth where stereotypes have been eliminated.

As the evening drew to an end, I told this riddle: "I travel through the sky, but I am not a plane or bird. I heal, but I am not a doctor. I provide food, but I am not a farmer. Who am I?"

They worked and worked in small groups to determine the answer. Finally, someone reported through the teacher, "No group can get all three, and the groups cannot agree on answers to all three, so you must preserve peace by telling us the answer before we go home to bed."

When he'd finished translating, the teacher waited for the answer. With arms folded across his thin chest and chin thrust forward, his posture showed that he shared the students' curiosity.

"I am Jesus," I said. "I heal the sick; I live in the heavens; I give food to eat. I am the answer to life's riddle."

We all had a good laugh, and then away they went. The teacher remained at the tent flap until the children's voices had faded into the night.

"Is it real?" he asked. "Is it really Jesus who heals and who lives in the sky and who sends us the food?"

"Yes. It is He who loves you and gives you all you need." I watched his face as I answered.

"And you came here to speak for Him?" His question was sincere, not angry or offended.

Jim answered in steady tones, "Yes, we believe He has sent us into the world to tell people about Him."

"Then it is true?" He turned to Jim. "It is really true He lives in the sky, He heals the sick, He sends the food, and you are His disciples?"

"Yes," we said together, looking at each other to see who should take the lead.

"You both believe it—He is for the white man and the black man?"

Ah, that was the point. The "white man's God" has some black skin.

"Then, if it is true, He can be my God. And you, my new friend, shall be my guru." With that declaration, he opened his neck bag, took out the picture of his former guru, and gave us a big hug. "Now, tell me about the books you carry."

We introduced him to the Bible, and, as the night wore on, he found solid faith in Jesus Christ. Can you imagine my joy when, one year later, I "bumped" into him on the trail from Beni? What are the odds of that happening? I tell you, my friend, that is God in action. He is the true God who sends us the food we need and who lives in the sky and who heals our diseases.

The true God does not tell us to kill those who do not believe as we do. He tells us to feed them. He tells us to bless them. He tells us to teach them what they will need to know for a better future. He is not afraid to be known by them. He is secure because He is true.

He said these signs would follow those who believe. They would be baptized, they would relieve the oppressed, they would speak in many languages, and they would minister healing; and nothing would harm them. (See Mark 16:17–18.)

These are the signs that follow true believers of a true God, and the greatest proof of the power of the truth is the transformation of people's lives. Jesus has made us ambassadors for healing, peace, and provision.

Ivana knew it. She became a believer and changed the course of the youth of her nation. And this young teacher knew it. He found the truth that night and went on to make believers of the future generation of his village. The Nepalese who stormed us for the books had found it, as had the arresting officers.

⌣

Bolstered by this thought, I thought of the mob surrounding us and their desperate need for truth—the truth that brings hope that never leaves room to be ashamed. In my heart, I cried out for them, and then it dawned on me that five hundred of them had received the truth that day.

I prayed that they would hide the Books, wander away from the fighting, and seek the truth in those pages. As we sat there wondering about our fate, my heart was encouraged at the thought of those young people believing in their hearts and moving from hatred to help.

Believers take action. Believers go out. Believers change nations.

# EIGHT

# THE HIGH HILLS

The high hills of North Thailand are refuge to a hodgepodge of humanity. The porous border and rough terrain make it a haven for drug traffickers. The fresh breezes make it a sanctuary from the dank heat of the deltas. The high places make it perfect for spiritualists of all kinds to try to get closer to the Creator through His creation.

We went there to find a monk.

A young lady in terrible torment had sought help from one of our friends. She had not slept for days. Her mind was filled with thoughts of suicide and grotesque figures. Her voice had changed, and her appearance was that of a modern zombie. Her unkempt hair was swept back to reveal a face developing deep lines of anguish.

She had lost consciousness several times, but a mandatory physical exam had found nothing out of the ordinary. Doctors were puzzled, psychiatrists bemused, psychologists befuddled; and now she came to those known as "believers in Jesus."

We received her and surrounded her with a team of women who could pray for her night and day. We began to call on the Lord for hope for her life and the ability to believe. The days were difficult, the nights terrifying.

As her mental stability began to return, she managed to sip some broth and energy drinks. Once we had restored her to physical balance, she began to speak more clearly. Over a period of three months, she told a fascinating story of hate, revenge, spiritism, and bondage. Some of it we immediately dismissed, only to later recall that she had shared those things with us. Her story taught us a great deal about the force of faith.

Well educated and highly regarded, she had worked as a business professional in the financial sector. She and her husband had been married for several years, and others regarded them as the model couple. Though they were not Christians and did not belong to a local church, they did believe in and fear the concept of a "god" in heaven. Their marriage and careers were developing beautifully, until the husband began traveling more and more frequently, and for longer periods of time, for business. Caught up in her career, and trusting him as she did, the wife did not investigate his absences for over a year. Then, at the suggestion of a friend, she began to ask questions upon his return from his latest trip. It took less than six months for her to figure out the truth: he was having an affair with another woman.

The discovery devastated her. Friends counseled her not to overreact, but she found this course impossible. Associates began to talk openly of her inability to keep her husband, and the sharks of the marketplace began to close in on her client base. Soon, her appearance began to change as the world of tormenting dreams crept into her sleeping hours and wreaked havoc on her slumber.

The thought occurred to her to go to a temple and ask the spirits to bring back her husband. She began to consult with temple mediums to gain the power to hold on to her husband. When these efforts failed to have any effect, the mediums said that she would have to go deeper into the spirit realm, because the power of the other woman was great. She drank potions, chanted curses, and made sacrifices to try to gain the upper hand, but to no avail. Frustrated, and deteriorating physically and mentally, she took leave of her business for a season in order to focus fully on this quest.

Through the mediums, she heard of a monk in South Thailand who had special powers in cases such as hers. But his services were costly, and they did not know how to contact him. She booked a flight to the city where the man was said to be located and began her search for him. Her appearance was a signboard of need. The local monks led her to mediums, who then led her to the man with the special powers.

She met with him several times, learning new chants, drinking new potions, and spending more money; but nothing worked. When she confronted the spiritist about his lack of efficacy, he replied that she needed to believe in him and in what they were doing—success was contingent upon her ability to believe. According to her testimony, she tried everything she could to believe that these efforts would work and that her husband would return. With her appetite gone, fasting was easy. The recommended sleep deprivation also came easily, as torment had taken her slumber.

After participating in ninety days of intensive sessions with the spiritist, and spending thousands of dollars in offerings, she was a skeleton. She had begun to take on the appearance of the spirits with which she had been communicating.

It was then that metal objects began to protrude from her skin. First, there would be a bump, and then a needle would emerge. This level of bondage is rare, even in Thai black magic. The spiritist began to withdraw from her; but, at her insistence, he agreed to enter into a blood covenant with her. They each drank the other's blood mixed with wine, then placed their hands on a ceremonial cloth dedicated for the ritual. The blood mingled, as did the spirits, and they were bound to each other.

Shortly after this ceremony, her friends had her committed for psychiatric evaluation. The doctor referred her to a pastor, and the case was passed to us, as our team included pastors and clinical psychologists from four nations. We agreed to take the case, which meant traveling to Kuala Lumpur, Malaysia. The pastor there was the lead, with the rest of us consulting and supporting in prayer.

The woman made slow, steady progress, beginning to take some food and get a little rest. Having no idea what her "right mind" would be, we just kept praying for the Lord to deliver her of all oppression. At times, she became violently angry and expressed a level of self-abuse and self-hatred that was, at best, alarming to us. Each of us went through periods of wondering why and how we had gotten into this case, but the Lord's love for her kept us working on it.

As the spirit webs of her tormented mind began to unravel, we could see a pathway of deliverance. We felt that her torment had begun in her inability to cope with being abandoned by her husband. When feelings of guilt had turned to self-loathing, she had opened her soul to torment. Her sense of personal failure was so profound that she had destroyed everything else in her life. She had become suicidal in every area: her job, her friendships, her family, her faith, and her body. She made frequent attempts to cut her wrists, but she always cut in the wrong direction, and never deep enough to hit an artery. As a result, we became encouraged; we felt that, deep in her heart, she did not want to die. Hope came with every onslaught.

Over the course of eighteen months, we concluded that we needed to follow the story from medium to medium and break the curse through the power of Jesus' name. This is how we started the search that would bring us to the hilltop of North Thailand.

The first several stops—local temples in Singapore—were very simple. Focused more on tourism than religious belief, the people we talked to remembered the case and said, as one, "South Thailand."

We met in North Malaysia and drove up to Thailand. Along the way, the woman began to have a desperate episode, so we had to slow our pace and encourage her to have the faith to face the torment in her soul. We searched the city. Yes, they knew of her; they also knew the man she had been meeting, but he was gone. His "temple" had been burned to the ground by a husband who had discovered that the medium had been using black magic against him. Some felt the spiritist had died in the fire; others were not sure.

After two days, we found a medium the woman recognized as having assisted in one of the events, and he directed us to North Thailand. The man we were looking for was building a new temple on one of the high hills there.

We flew to Chiang Mai, got a couple of vehicles, and recruited a translator named Leck to aid in our communication with the hill tribes. He was a pastor among the Karen hill tribe and a solid believer in Jesus. We drove there in two vehicles, with someone always watching the woman for any sign of recognition in the spirit. Amazingly, she slept well on the trip. It seemed that the closer we got to the man, the calmer she became. Fearing that she would slip into a deep trance, we tried to balance her with conversation.

We arrived in the town around eleven in the morning. Immediately we took a walk to see if we could find a contact to the man. The place was filled with people of all nationalities—Chinese who had fled to freedom, hippies from the world over, Thai and Burmese, and the local hill tribes. At a church, we found a Chinese pastor who told us of a very strong medium who came from the South and appeared to have quite a bit of money. He showed us the location of the new facility the man was building and said that many of his church members, as well as those of other churches, had begun to believe in the man. This fellow, he said, was very powerful in the ancient arts of Thai black magic, and already it was said in the villages that many of those who opposed him had become violently ill, some to the point of death.

We thanked the Chinese pastor, then went to find this man, following his directions. It was a beautiful day in one of the world's most spectacular places. The air was so clear that it made an impression upon us. We were on peaks several hundred feet above the valleys, with a view of the hillsides covered with verdant foliage. Multicolored parrots sped from tree to tree, and the sound of songbirds filled the crisp, clean air. Only one little cloud clung to the valley floor. It had somehow escaped the morning's heat, perhaps shaded from the sun or fed by a bamboo cluster.

The monk was building quite the facility. He had money indeed. About twenty novitiates were there to serve him. The main building was made of steel and sheet metal. They were constructing the altar, and it was immense. The idol had not yet been made; but the base on which it would stand measured 20 by 10 meters. This man had a following somewhere.

Leaving the lady in the van with two women, we went and asked for the monk. Probably hopeful for a generous offering from some Westerners, he came toward us with the sheepish smile common to Asian beggars. With hands extended and then elevated, as if in prayer, he greeted each member of our team. When he reached me, he asked Leck who we were and what we wanted. We had instructed Leck to tell him that I was a fat holy man from the West who had heard of his powers and had come to exchange some fortune-telling with him. The young man was to say that I had a "word" for this man, and that I felt that he would have a "word" for me; we were hoping for a face-to-face meeting in the spirit.

The monk was happy to oblige, and we sat down together for tea. I suggested he go first. He went into a trance and then told me that I was great in the spirit, had good karma, was free to walk throughout Asia, and would not have trouble, but that I should watch out for the Arabs, as they would try to kill me.

When it was my turn, I looked deep into his eyes and then spoke in tongues. After a few minutes, when he had crossed over from feeling nervous to realizing something real was happening, I took his hand in mine. Then I told him that he had been having a recurring dream. He could see the end of the age was coming. He could see the devastation, and a face kept appearing to him. He did not know the name of the person. The face had been beaten, the forehead cut, as if with thorns. Blood flowed on the face.

He knew in his spirit that if he could call the name of the man with the bleeding face, he would be saved from the fires that were consuming everything. But he was awakened without knowing the name.

I asked him if this was true, and he said yes.

Then, still holding his right hand in mine, I told him I knew the name and had been sent to tell it to him. I asked if he wanted to know the name. He said that he did.

I told him that once he knew this name, he could no longer call upon any other name—that this was the only name he could ever call, or else he would perish in the fires he had seen.

I asked again if he wanted to know the name.

Yes, of course he did. At this point, his eyes were twitching, and he was beginning to sweat.

Leck positioned himself close to the man. Still holding his hand, I leaned forward and told him that the man he had seen—the man who could save him from the fire; the man with the piercing eyes and the blood flowing from His face—was none other than Jesus.

When Leck said the name "Jesus," several things happened. The monk pulled his hand free from mine, then struck the young pastor twice across the face before jumping to his feet and cursing us. He stormed about the place, screaming, "Never say that name! Never say that name!"

Trying to light a cigarette, he dismissed the young students, and then, in a complete rage, he started for the two of us. The wind began to blow, and suddenly, over the edge of the mountain, came the little cloud. Now a great whirlwind, it swept through the place where we were. It blew away every loose thing, and several people from our group and all of the young monks fell to their knees in fear. The power was like nothing I have ever seen.

Leck, on his knees, offered this prayer: "Father, forgive him."

The monk ran to his house and cursed us from inside. Feeling that the power had been driven from him, we left.

Our next stop was the hilltop temple of the king of Thailand. We went there and prayed for the beautiful country. During this time, three gangsters came to confront the Karen pastor (Leck). They threatened his life if we returned. At peace with it all, we left.

The next morning, a pastor in Chiang Mai came to greet us. He had heard about the whirlwind and wanted to show us the morning newspaper. At exactly the same time, powerful winds had blown through Chiang Mai. The newspaper article went on to say that strange occurrences such as whirlwinds had blown throughout the northeastern section of Thailand.

In the years that followed, revival has come to the villages in those areas. Many miracles have happened—in particular, curses and Thai black magic have been stopped.

The woman has been healed. She does not look like she did during her years of torment. Those who know her say she is more radiant a person that she has ever been. Her husband has not returned, and he may never return; but, through the power of the name of Jesus, she is free.

The young pastor who took the hit continues to disciple those who believe.

The monk was gunned down by gangsters several months later.

⌒

Gunfire is the last futility of man in expressing his desire to control. It was true in Thailand, and it is true in Aceh. When the guns come out, reason has stopped.

In our situation, things were becoming unreasonable.

# NINE

# THE WALLS WERE BEGINNING TO CLOSE IN ON US

T he walls were beginning to close in on us. Accustomed to walking about, I was beginning to feel the need to stretch my legs. To the left of the cell was an open court measuring about three square meters; it had a sink and some buckets, and was obviously the custodian's washroom. Leaving the enclosure, I walked out into this area, only to hear more clearly the sounds of the conflict outside. We had been about an hour-and-a-half into the event, and the crowd had not lost any of its fury. A barrage of stones and bottles flew into the courtyard, and I realized that the open roof made it a possible point of access to our refuge. As I stepped quickly back inside, I thought of believers I know who have spent long times in such places.

I thought of Alan Yuan. In the far western regions of China, Alan had spent twenty years in a labor camp so bleak that there were no walls; the guards told the prisoners that they could leave whenever they wanted to. But there was no surviving an escape into the Turkmen Desert, which surrounded the camp.

I also thought of Wang Ming Dao and his twenty-two-year-and-ten-month "honeymoon" with Jesus. Like Alan's, Wang's crime had been refusing to sign allegiance to the Communist Party in China. He had thought of suicide, but the Lord had preserved him.

I thought of our own previous arrests, in China, Nepal, Mongolia, and Russia, and how the Lord had always come through for us.

Then my mind recalled Pastor Mai, a dear friend from Vietnam. With the fall of Saigon, and the formation of Communist reeducation programs, all the South Vietnamese who believed in Jesus had to renounce their faith or, at the very least, agree to not spread the gospel. In Saigon City, there was a group of young seminarians with divergent opinions on the expedient thing to do. One group recalled a proverb that captured the essence of Ecclesiastes 9:4, "*A live dog is better off than a dead lion*" (NIV). Through their efforts, the church, though severely compromised, was recognized by the government. Although they were not able to grow their church during the occupation, they were able to outlast the oppression and survive.

A second group of Vietnamese Christians thought it best to go underground and resist as long as they could. This group was led by four young men who had experienced the Pentecostal baptism in the Holy Spirit. The members of this group had their differences with those of the first group, who viewed this underground church as fanatic and extreme. Problems arose when the legitimized church supplied the authorities with information concerning the underground group. Which pressures were applied to exact that information, we do not know; but the four founding members of the underground church were sought, arrested, and tortured, in an effort to force them to deny their faith and sign with the party. None of them ever did.

Pastor Mai was one of those men. Branded as a rebel, and having his church closed, Mai began to meet in a home with seventeen others, including his own family. To avoid detection, they changed the meeting location often. They had an intense love for worship, for the Bible, and for each other. The pressures of the day formed the crucible from which they would eventually emerge indivisible.

Eventually, someone whose identity is yet unknown informed the authorities about the group and their meetings. Once again, the police took Mai in for questioning.

When he refused to cooperate, they resorted to less humane means of interrogation. They tried solitary confinement, but Mai would not give up the members of his new church. The authorities beat him and denied him both food and sleep, but he would not give the names. So, in frustration, they tied his hands behind his back and hung him from a peg in the wall in a completely dark room. And they left him there, to break or to die.

The pain never let up. Mai cried out to the Lord in tongues with every waking moment. Days went by. The guards listened as the shouting become more and more muffled, until it was no more than a murmur. They declared him insane and threw him into an alley behind the jail, thinking he would surely die. His arms were severely damaged from the torture, and he was dehydrated. He somehow made it to a doorway and was able to drink what little water he could find on the streets. Eventually, Mai made his way home, into the loving arms of his wife and home church, where he recuperated.

I was introduced to him by a mutual friend. We had prayed our way through Vietnam and had arrived in Saigon on our way back to Singapore. My friend arranged the meeting, telling them that I, too, had been arrested several times for my faith. He also told them about the South East Asia Prayer Center and our commitment to local house church movements.

When I met Mai, we became fast friends. I was invited to return the following year to teach at a leaders' retreat to be held at a beachfront location. Honored beyond imagination, I set my schedule by that meeting.

On the first day of the retreat, I was standing in the gentle surf with a Vietnamese pastor a few years my junior. As the waves gently swept the sand from our legs, he reached into the water and deftly retrieved a long strand of kelp. After biting off a section for himself, he offered the rest to me. In like fashion to his, I bit off a big piece and then handed it back to him. Amazed, he took another bite, grinning as he chewed. Not to be put off, I repeated the process, which continued until he indicated he had eaten enough.

"Where you meet Mai?" he asked, while chewing the last mouthful.

"Friend of a friend," I answered.

"We meet in jail," he went on, satisfied with my knowledge of the standard house-church answer.

"He told me about Jesus," he continued, looking up the beach toward the pastor. "He a good man; led many to Jesus."

That evening, under the cover of a netted canopy strung between palm trees, I heard some of the most fascinating testimonies of believers. Most of the key leaders there had come to Christ while in prison. They were people who had worked for, or been related in some way to, the Americans. It had been assumed that they were collaborators in the counterrevolution; they had been imprisoned on political grounds and had been mixed in with the four Christian leaders.

One by one, they shared their stories of release; of sharing the gospel; of being arrested again; of reeducation—and of starting the entire cycle all over again. Men and women shared with candor about their extreme faith in Jesus. My own level of belief paled in the light of their passion.

It became clear that night that one believer, suspended from a wall and left to die, had resulted in the conversion of forty thousand people; and that those people were closely knit, traveling throughout Vietnam carrying the good news of Jesus Christ.

We were joined by a young woman they called the "Lion of Da Nang." She was the daughter so many of them had lost. She had just been released from a Haiphong jail after being arrested for preaching Christianity. How did they know she was from Da Nang? Her accent. A policeman had overheard her asking for directions; realizing she was not local, he had brought her to the local station to find out where she was from and what she was doing out of her area. She was identified by her previous record and then spent a month in jail. She was most animated as she shared testimony after testimony of those imprisoned with her who had come to Christ. The Lord had turned her difficult situation into a time of harvest and victory. She had not felt fear at all.

I was reminded of Peter being identified as a Galilean by the little girl at the fireside on the night of Christ's arrest and how he had tried to deny his association with Him. This young woman had reversed the tables. She was so very bold. The group contemplated her next trip and decided to send her farther north, to the Chinese border, to confirm the reports they had heard from that area.

The next matter of discussion was the criteria for the title of "full-time worker." For them, this involved the selling of one's home and land, giving the proceeds to the treasury of the work, and then striking out by faith to plant a church where there was none.

⌣

As I remembered all of this, I looked around at our team. Sure, we were committed to Christ. Yes, of course we believed enough to hear from Him and obey what He was asking us to do. But which one of us could take the steps those Vietnamese Christians had taken? I was humbled then, and I am humbled now. Their commitment has kept the flame of faith burning brightly through an otherwise dark day in the life of the church in Asia. They expressed, under the cover of darkness, a level of commitment I had never known. My embarrassment had grown as I realized that, after all of their reports, I was to share my faith with them.

Despite the rattle of gunfire, the gun locker in the hallway, the smell of the gun smoke, and the sound of the helicopter in the air, my mind was not in Indonesia in 1999; it was clearly in Vietnam twenty-five years prior. Mai had "survived," and so would we. The Lion of Da Nang had "survived," and so would we. And if the Lord was going to allow us to be tortured, then we would join with a happy group afterward to share the fellowship of His suffering.

Leck had said of the blow to his face, "I thank God that He has counted me worthy to suffer today for His name's sake. I ask Him to forgive the man and save his soul."

Ivana had prayed daily for the schoolmaster who had tried to commit her to a painful death. One day, she explained to me, "We do not hate the Russians any more than our parents hated the Germans. We pray for them; and, should the Lord desire that we must suffer to draw closer to Him, then we thank God for the honor to suffer in His name."

There was a sound of a group of people coming down the hallway. I looked at the Banker. He held up five fingers.

All I could think was, *What will this be?*

# PART III:

*"Be wise as serpents and harmless as doves."*
—Matthew 10:16

*Behold, I send you out as sheep in the midst of wolves. Therefore be wise as serpents and harmless as doves. But beware of men, for they will deliver you up to councils and scourge you in their synagogues. You will be brought before governors and kings for My sake, as a testimony to them and to the Gentiles. But when they deliver you up, do not worry about how or what you should speak. For it will be given to you in that hour what you should speak; for it is not you who speak, but the Spirit of your Father who speaks in you. Now brother will deliver up brother to death, and a father his child; and children will rise up against parents and cause them to be put to death. And you will be hated by all for My name's sake. But he who endures to the end will be saved. When they persecute you in this city, flee to another. For assuredly, I say to you, you will not have gone through the cities of Israel before the Son of Man comes. A disciple is not above his teacher, nor a servant above his master. It is enough for a disciple that he be like his teacher, and a servant like his master. If they have called the master of the house Beelzebub, how much more will they call those of his household! Therefore do not fear them. For there is nothing covered that will not be revealed, and hidden that will not be known.*
—Matthew 10:16–26

# TEN

# IT WAS A SMALL GROUP

I t was a small group: the slight man with the gun in his waistband, the
man in uniform, and the small man with a round head. They were
polite; they asked if we were alright, and assured us that the situation had
intensified.

The small, round-headed man was introduced as an officer from Interpol. He
was professional and stood with the air of authority one would expect.

"Mr. Mark," he said, before going into an explanation that has stuck with
me all through these years. "This has become an international situation. I am
certain that when you arrived, you had no idea where you were or what was happening here. I am sure you understand more about it now. Because you are from
the USA, this situation has very strong international implications. Eventually,
your government will become involved, as well as the government of your friend.
Please cooperate with these men in every way. They are professionals and will
help you in this situation. We will be in contact with your governments to assure
them of your safety and to answer any questions they may have. I am sure that,
with your cooperation, this matter can be resolved."

The slight man was next. He had changed into a black shirt while the other
man was speaking. He had the build of a Siamese cat, with no excess fat on his

body. His eyes even resembled a cat's, seeming to peer through mine into my soul as he stood before me and spoke.

"Mr. Mark." His speech was gentle. "I am what we in the police call a 'Ninja.' This is a term used for those who are authorized to use our bodies as weapons, and who can kill without having to ask permission. We answer to no one. It is my job to see that you and your friends are not killed. The people outside have demanded that you be turned over to them. Then you would be tortured, torn limb from limb, and dragged through the streets. They honestly hate you.

"Do not worry. You will be alright. Just do exactly as we say. It is our job to protect you, and we will. I am going out to talk with them and get them to see that you are not worth dying for."

As he left, the man in uniform stepped up. His calm was my joy.

"Mr. Mark, I am in charge of the uniformed police and the military involved in this international situation. Did you hear the sound of the helicopter? We tried to fly a chopper in here to take you out, but when it approached the area, someone in the crowd lifted a surface-to-air device. Thankfully, it was spotted, and the chopper withdrew, or they would have shot it down. If that had happened, they would have gained the courage to rush the building and kill us all. This is a very serious situation.

"It is no longer important whether or not you knew the situation here. What is important now is that we get you and my people out of here alive. The power to the station has been cut. Your car has been burned. The rioters have gained access to the building two times.

"We are having commandos come to rescue us. It will take at least forty-five minutes for them to get here. Please stay away from the windows and follow any orders we give you."

As they went to their respective stations, we all looked at the Banker. He was holding up six fingers. We smiled at each other and took our places of waiting. There was no talk, no verbal prayer. It was unlike any other life-threatening situation I had ever experienced. We all were filled with a resolute calm.

It was then that I realized I was prepared to meet Jesus. *I could be a martyr of the faith in just a couple of hours*, I thought, as I turned back to my waiting place.

Other people had threatened to kill me before. There was the wife-beater who came to my office with the .357 Magnum and threatened to blow my brains out if I didn't tell him where his wife was. I refused. He didn't kill me, then or later, when he got out of jail.

There was the Catholic priest in Guatemala who assured me that I would be dead in the morning if another young person prayed with me to receive Jesus.

But those experiences had taken place quickly; this was taking a lot of time. It gave me a chance to prepare my heart. Jesus began to prepare me, as He has all those who have been sent out by Him. He promised, "After the Holy Ghost is come upon you, you will receive power to be martyrs for Me." (See Acts 1:8.)

I returned to my corner of the room and felt that sweet presence come upon me. Again, there was no fear, just looking forward to the chapters of the plan of God as they would unfold in my life.

# ELEVEN

# *"LOVE YOUR ENEMIES"*

Jesus said, *"Love your enemies"* (Matthew 5:44; Luke 6:27, 35). Were these Indonesians, so hungry for our blood, really our enemies? Had we not instigated the whole thing? How was I to feel about a couple of thousand people who wanted to cut me limb by limb and drag me through the streets?

Did they represent all Muslims? Were they frustrated with the world's imbalance of wealth? Were they that fearful of three middle-aged men and a youth? Was America that bad, really? Were they under the influence of evil spirits? Were we pawns in an international opportunity to be on CNN? These thoughts and more flooded my mind as I sat down to wait out the next chapter.

Level six—the Banker had indicated we had reached level six. I realized a new, keen awareness of sounds. There was a discernible calm among us. The Doctor's veins were calm; and, without the driver's nervousness, we could almost take a nap. We shared tense smiles, raised eyebrows, and shoulder shrugs all around, and gave our guide a gentle smile. It is all in a day's work for those sent out by the Lord. We were a team. There were no divisions. We had been called of the Lord to share a common experience, and, while it was not what we'd had in mind in the morning, it made for a very interesting afternoon.

*"Love your enemies."* Christian maturity is seen in this simple sentence, and I rested my drifting mind on its anchor. Could a person who was going to kill you be seen as your enemy?

〜

We had walked for three days along the Dudh Kosi River in the Terai region of the Royal Kingdom of Nepal. It was hot, and the torrential rains that fell did nothing to cool the temperature. Our team of four Westerners and four Nepalese had been dropped off by a truck in the middle of the night. We turned upriver the next morning and had been walking ever since. We had completed seventeen river crossings and had spent hours sloshing along through flooded rice paddies. Our first night, we had aroused a horse from her bedding place, only to lose to her countermove around three in the morning. We had blisters. We were hungry and had no good food. We had nineteen days of uphill trekking ahead of us, and we were not in a good mood.

Eventually, we were befriended by a dashing young leader on horseback. He led us to his family's grain mill, where we enjoyed a midday nap and some fresh water. With only four hours to go, we headed into the town of Gaighat, in the Sagarmatha Zone of eastern Nepal. This little town had a school and food, and we were glad to reach it. The children from a local school lightened our bags of several copies of *Who Is Jesus?* Everyone was happy.

Everyone except for a lawyer standing across the street. He made a beeline for one of the kids, seized the book, and headed for the police. Our team took a vote and decided to sit it out in a tea shop. We got some rice and had started refilling our empty tanks when the commotion began. The lawyer was back, this time with the law. Eight of us went in eight directions as quickly as we could. They decided to follow me. It was a good choice; I was the oldest, the fattest, and the slowest of the team.

I was fine until hitting a hill, which, in Nepal, can be found about every fifty meters. Our guide/translator was with me. Maybe they wanted to talk to him, and I was just in the bargain. The policeman put his hand on my shoulder and spoke, his voice soft: "Would you come with me, please?"

I have since learned that the gentleness with which this is said does not always indicate the strength of the person saying it. Some very big policemen have very gentle voices.

I turned slowly and submitted to his direction. He was tall and appeared to be in his early twenties. He also seemed thrilled to have done his duty to preserve public security. Not a bad kid, he wanted to practice his English, so we selected the subject of basketball and worked on the related vocabulary. I am often amazed at the penetration of professional sports around the world. People who do not know about flush toilets can tell you who won last year's NBA Slam Dunk Contest. And in the days of Michael Jordan, the world was awash in Nike imitations. Every police outpost I have visited, from Siam to Siberia, has featured a tattered basketball hoop, and this one was no exception. This young man could never be called my "enemy."

As we approached the building housing the municipal court and the chief district officer's office, the young man stopped me for a formal briefing. "This man you are about to meet is the Chief District Officer. He holds the power of life and death over everyone who lives here. When we go in, I will bow down on the floor before him to show respect. You must bow down, also, and wait for him to tell you to get up. Do not raise your eyes before he tells you to do so."

*Now we are approaching someone who has too high a self-image,* I thought. *Hell will freeze over before I bow down to any "Chief District Officer" in this time-forgotten, hole-in-the-wall town.*

We entered an austere room, and, sure enough, the policeman hit the floor, on his knees in front of the desk. I smiled courteously and extended my hand to the man whom I would come to love.

"Rise," he said to the policeman, who seemed amazed that I was standing. "Stand by," he added to the young man.

*Good,* I thought. *He is a man of few words. Now he will tell me something, and I will leave, and that will be the end of that.*

"Mr. Mark." His English was tinged with a British accent. His eyes rose from my passport. "You have caused me a big problem today. Has our officer informed you as to my rank and title in this district? You know that this is my district and that I hold the power of life and death here? Your future is in my hands. Please come and sit here." He turned to a servant. "Bring us some tea." Then to me, "Would you like a biscuit?"

When he said, "That will be all," the room emptied of everyone else but the police officer and the servant, who brought tea and biscuits and made us most comfortable. I began to like this man. Maybe he had to put up such a fierce front to keep the locals in check. I had no idea, but the gentleman was much nicer than the life-and-death king.

"Now, as I say," he continued, "you have caused me a big problem today. Do you know that Nepal is a Hindu country? That is to say that everyone in Nepal is a Hindu, and our king is descended from a Hindu god."

I had no idea about any such thing. There are Buddhists and there are Muslims and there are Christians, so I thought his point of view to be pretty narrow. Seeing the question in my eyes, he continued his explanation.

"All Nepalese are registered. If you are born in a Hindu family, then you are Hindu. If you are born in a Buddhist family, then you are Buddhist. Do you understand?"

Not waiting for an answer, he continued. "Did you know that to change one's religion, you have to reregister, and you could spend one year in jail? Did you know that when you reregister, you must supply the name of the person who convinced you to change religion, and that person must spend three years in jail? And did you know that if you change your religion to Christianity and you are baptized in water, you must spend six years in jail, and the person who persuades you to be baptized must spend six years in jail for every person?"

"I did not know," I answered.

"I thought you did not know, so I got you this copy of our law in English, so that you would not be ignorant of the law. Please tell me what you did last night."

"I had some rotten rice, ate a piece of cheese, and slept." I sipped my tea.

"Yes, but before that, you told two hundred Nepalese to repeat a prayer and change their religion, and you gave them a book. And, because you are a white Westerner, these innocent people believed you and prayed with you, and now they all want to reregister as Christians. You have given me a big problem. You must go to jail for three years per person, or a total of six hundred years." Now he was not smiling. "Now, tell me, why did you come here?" He sat back to listen to the only defense I could give in the face of evidence and a clear case of proselytizing.

"Sir," I began with respect, after a deep draught of tea to clean my tightening throat, "it was never my intention to cause you any problem. Actually, the problem began when you arrested me. If I had not been arrested, there would be no problem; but, to the bigger question: Why did I come here? I am a believer in

Jesus Christ. He is the love of God demonstrated for all men. He has asked us to go into all the earth to tell everyone that if they will believe in Him, they will have eternal life. If they call upon His name, they will be saved. I found this to be true in my life. I was caught in sins that I could not defeat through discipline or self-control. I called upon the Lord, and He heard me and delivered me from this sin. It is His love that compels us to go to every man and give him the opportunity to be saved.

"Look at me, sir. I am too old for this trekking, and I am not at all fit for it; but, because Jesus loves you, I have walked all this way.

"Jesus knows who you are. Jesus knows where you are. And Jesus knows what you need. Because He loves you, He has sent us here to tell you. He probably controlled even our arrest so that you might know that He loves you.

"It is not as if we had chosen Nepal to the exclusion of others. We have walked in many nations and will walk in still more, if you allow it, to tell people about Jesus and His great love for them."

Having delivered the message, I sat back and watched his face.

"This," he said, "gives me a really big problem. I am the law in this district. All my people know that; there is no question. You have broken the law. If I put you in jail, your country will come and get you, and my people will say I bowed the knee to the US. If I do not put you in jail, my people will say I am a weak ruler and I bowed my knee to the foreigner. This is a big problem. What am I to do with you?"

Silence is a great defense. I looked at him with true compassion for his dilemma.

"I could just have my men take you out to a cliff, throw you off, and report you as a trekking accident. We have those here every year."

We shared some more tea and glucose biscuits as he read the "evidence" taken by the lawyer. He was intent on unraveling the dilemma, and I saw no need to interrupt his study. Finally, he straightened his desktop, leaned forward in his chair, and fixed his eyes on mine.

"I have decided to show you grace. I will let you go if you promise that you will not share this book with any more people in my district."

He seemed satisfied, so I got out my map to see where the end of his district was. It was a two-day walk for me; one day for his young policeman, who was going to go with us, to be certain no local person tried to bother us with conversation. With a deal struck, we had more tea, and our team spent the night with company from the police force.

We trekked on through Nepal and found great receptivity for the message we carried. I met wonderful policemen and military along the way. We got to stay in the police station in two towns and a military jail in a third. It was eye-opening.

The following year, I was approached by a local Christian leader during a visit to Kathmandu. He had heard of my arrest and zeal for the gospel, and he excitedly shared with me a clipping from the Kathmandu newspaper. The Chief District Officer of the town of Gaighat had been struck dead by a bolt of lightning out of a clear blue sky. Local believers had seen it as a sign from heaven, and, caught up in the idea, I began using it as a lesson for those who would hinder the servants of God.

Six months later, while preparing to share this story, I was reminded of the love the Lord had for this man, whose task it had been to prevent others from becoming Christians, yet who had arranged for my release from prison. God's timing was perfect—permitting my arrest so that I could share His love with that Chief District Officer before his death that very year.

The power of life and death was not with the man with the title; it was with the One who gave His life that all might live.

Perhaps it was the remark by the "Ninja" of how he had the right to kill, or the comment of the police and military concerning our outcome, but this memory brought me great joy. It has always kept at the forefront of my mind Matthew 5:44: *"Love your enemies,...and pray for those which despitefully use you, and persecute you"* (KJV).

# TWELVE

# THE ONES WHO
# ARE OUR ENEMIES

B ut you could not understand—*somos pobres* [we will always be poor]."

Hector's words cut to my heart. In Spanish, there are two verbs for "to be," *estar* and *ser*. *Estar* is often used to express something that is temporary, such as in the phrase, "We are tired" (*estamos cansados*); *ser*, on the other hand, is used to describe more permanent situations, such as in the phrase "We are men" (*somos hombres*). *Ser* is used to enforce permanent characteristics of people—who they are; their very being; something that would never change. Hector, along with his people, grew up speaking and believing that poverty was part of his identity.

We stood on the rim of La Limonada, a Guatemalan barrio famous for crime, and the largest Latin American urban slum outside of Brazil. "These people do not want to do drugs, they do not want to steal, and they certainly do not want to die young; but that is life for us, and it will never change. We do not have one drop of hope that it will ever change.

"Brother Mark," he continued with a smile, "you love us. We can feel that you love us. You can walk anywhere down there and be safe because the people know you love them. But other people who come here—the fat cats and rich—they are the ones who are our enemies. They keep us living like this through the power of their money and corruption. They control the drugs and the crime. They take the youngest kids and make them addicts, thieves, prostitutes, and murderers. Then they treat us like the filth they have caused us to become.

"If one of them ever comes down here, he would be killed for his shoes. Brother, we are born to this, and we will die to it. The rich and powerful will never allow this system to change. They are the enemies of their own people. There is no changing the fact of one's name. When I give my two-name name to an employer, the job is gone. When I give my name, people know I have no father, and the doors of opportunity are closed.

"Brother, we have a caste system here, even in the church. If you and I go to a meeting, everyone will want to be near you because you are from North America and I am from La Limonada. You will be invited in, but I will be asked to stay outside. You will be free to talk with anyone in the room; I cannot. It is a way of life for us. We accept it. It is the system. It will not change for us. Not now, not ever."

〜

Was this how they felt out in that street? Was this the fire that burned in the Irate Imam and the man in the ball cap? Was this why they shook with the desire to kill and talked about cutting off our limbs and dragging us through the streets? Had the crumbs of the tilted table so offended them that they were willing to risk their own lives just to become somebody else?

I began to understand as I listened to their chanting from my safe waiting place.

"Love your friends and hate your enemy" was the message of the culture.

"Get even for what they have done to you."

"They think they are superior, but they do not recognize our culture."

"They do not recognize the prophet; death to the infidels!"

These were the logs on the fire. But had the spark that ignited them been something deeper?

〜

On that afternoon in Guatemala, I had forced my young friend into my truck, and we had driven to the National Palace. With him in tow, I used all of my white North American courage and walked right past the guards and into the foyer. I took the steps two a time, reaching the reception room of the president before anyone could stop me. Hector stayed close to me, and he was amazed when I opened the door and said to the guard, "Turn on the lights."

Still in shock, he obeyed when I summoned him to the platform holding the president's chair and had him sit in the forbidden seat of power. The guard looked a bit surprised when I handed him a camera and asked him to take a photo, one that will forever be in my memory. I told Hector, "Jesus has caused us to sit in heavenly places high above all principalities and powers." (See Ephesians 1:21; 2:6.)

My young friend had just learned the first lesson of loving your enemies: Do not have any enemies.

For the next twenty years, Hector battled to rise above the racial discrimination into which he had been born. The injustices have been many. I have watched roomfuls of people completely ignore him. This man, who has founded churches, given huge sums of money to the poor, established and run his own business, and raised three children as a widower, all while supporting his mother and an invalid sister, is often treated as a lesser being by people born in a different zone or country. I have seen the pain in his heart and the agony on his face as he watches others of lowly estate become the downtrodden masses of humanity.

⌒

Was this the fuel for the cry in the streets of Aceh that day? As I sat thinking in my cell, I realized that just as the Guerrilla Army of the Poor would load a group of gunmen into a pickup truck and chase medical care from their community, so would the Irate Imam and the man in the T-shirt chase financial investments, medicine, and education from theirs. They would rather be sick, dumb, and poor than have to sit any longer under the rich man's table. Social reform was the cry in the streets, and they felt that Allah would give it to them, as long as they rid the place of infidels and those who offered them sanctuary.

Were they the "enemy"?

Was I the "enemy"?

We were talking about killing. The "Ninja," whose right to kill was the result of our presence there, would represent us. Who would die first because of us?

One does not normally come to a religious debate armed with a surface-to-air weapon. This thing had deeper roots. Why would a man put on an "I Love America" T-shirt or a silly-looking baseball cap and then lecture me on religion? What was going on here? Was it an uprising in the centuries-old ethnic dispute of the Acehnese and the Javanese? Why the reference to Ambon, where Christians and Muslims were slaughtering each other every night in the name of their god?

Who was the "enemy"?

I have faced death many times. No stranger to the feel of its presence, I am very alert when it is around. Someone was likely to die this day. Someone was likely to be slain as an "enemy," which is to say, a person taking the opposite position. It could be me; but it would probably be some kid who decided to challenge the "Ninja," or someone who got in the way when the commandos came to get us.

⌒

In my first year as a missionary, I contracted malaria from some little mosquito. That disease became my life-threatening enemy. We fought it with medicine, blankets, rubbing alcohol, and all that goes into the war against this enemy. I lost weight, became violently ill, was confined to bed, and vomited at the smell of food. Fevers and chills took turns possessing my body.

Outside our group home was a Spanish man. I later came to know that his name was Felipe Gonzales. He was born in Guatemala and was pastor to the youth of Guatemala City who lived in La Limonada. When he heard I was sick, he began fasting and praying for my healing. Each day, he came to walk and pray in front of the house where I was being treated. As he passed by, he would touch the door and the doorbell but wouldn't knock or ring.

One day, our young teammate Jonathan said, "This man comes every day, but he does not knock. Should I ask him in?"

"Certainly," I said, wondering what this would be about.

Felipe entered the room apologetically and asked general questions about my health, my family, and so forth. Finally I asked him if he would pray for me.

"Me, pray for you?" he asked.

"Yes, please, would you pray for me?" I responded, not realizing that he had never felt worthy to pray for a white missionary.

As he prayed, I felt warmth cover my entire body. Something healing touched me, and within a week, I was in wonderful shape. The malaria was gone and has never returned.

What had been the "enemy"? Was this man so culture-bound that I could have lain there and died without his prayers? Had we done this to him?

There is an enemy. He is ready to add fuel to any burning offense. He will always couch his deceptions in religious jargon or spiritual terminology. He comes to rob, hurt, kill, and destroy. (See John 10:10.) People are taken captive by his ways when they harbor resentment or when they are oppressed by the belief that they are lesser or inferior. Often, they feel as the disciples did, confident that someday, a deliverer will come who will lift the heel of the oppressor—be it an oil company, the existing government, or a religious hierarchy—from their throat. The disciples of Jesus wanted to be free from Rome. They wanted a kingdom to be established on the earth, in which they would sit to the right and left of the King and rule over their former oppressors. This was their dream, and when it looked as though Jesus would not bring it to fruition, they all fled. They ran away. They were scattered by the crushing of their false hope.

But Jesus came to give them victory over the one who was the enemy of their souls. Not distracted by economics or politics, Jesus kept His focus on the task before Him. He suffered the cross, taking the hatred of every man—even those in the streets of Aceh, the "Ninja," the Irate Imam, and the Hat.

When Jesus rose from the dead, He defeated the real enemy. Is it any wonder that those who teach "an eye for an eye" also teach that Jesus did nothing significant on the cross? Is it any wonder that those who teach "a tooth for a tooth," "a limb for a limb," and avenging one's position in life also teach that there is no resurrection from the dead? They insist that Jesus stayed in the grave after His death on the cross, and that His disciples must have faked His resurrection. Is it any wonder that instead of teaching young men to heal, they teach them to kill?

No, those in the street were not the enemy.

The guards at the palace were not the enemy.

The door and the doorbell were not the enemy.

The enemy is the spirit that turns man against fellow man. It is the spirit that does not see the value of each individual. It is the one who robs, hurts, kills, and destroys. Jesus is the One who came that we might have life, and have it more abundantly. (See John 10:10.) That means we can sit in His chair. That means there is healing for all. That means we should have an open heart to every man. That means striving for unity, not divisions, among men.

# THIRTEEN

# THE "DOMINOES" WILL FALL

T he 'dominoes' will fall in Latin America. The same way Communism has swept through Europe and is sweeping through Asia, it will now sweep through Latin America until the hammer and sickle rest on American shores!"

This was the mantra of the masses as we entered Guatemala. Their only hope was found in land reform. The native peoples demanded the right to rule themselves and be free from the "Yankee oppressors." The memories of Che Guevara and Fidel Castro were the only hope for the miserable multitudes. First would be Nicaragua, then El Salvador and Honduras, and then Guatemala, before the big prize—Mexico.

As if sparked by this cacophony of false hope, the earth began to shake. It shook violently for about thirty-five seconds. The epicenter of the earthquake was in an arid valley on the small Motagua River, which carries what little rain falls on the dry side of the continental divide as it winds its way through the former Mayen wonderland now known as Guatemala. From side to side and up and down, the earth opened and swallowed up the lives of fifty thousand people in just thirty-five seconds.

Survivors tell stories of dogs that wandered out into the streets and dropped dead from shock. It was as if God had picked up a corner of the earth's surface and given it a hard shake. Women became widows, children became orphans, and villages became graveyards in that instant. Hopes and dreams were shattered, and politics went out the window with the screams of those trapped beneath mountains of rubble.

One of those trapped was Lazuro Ochoa Catalan. "Don Lacho," as he was affectionately known in his village, was an old man. He was from the Catalan/Mayen family line that had lived on the southern rim of the Motagua Valley for generations. Unlike the shorter, broader, dark-eyed Mayens, these descendants of the conquistadores were tall, with green or brown eyes and fair skin. Don Lacho had been asleep when the dark village had shaken. He was struck in the head by a terra cotta tile from the roof, which had caved in, trapping him beneath the rubble in a growing pool of his own blood. Dazed, he began to lose hope of lasting through that fateful night.

Hector Zetino was a fatherless teenager who lived in a shack of corrugated tin perched on a steep hillside in one of the barrios of impoverished multitudes in Guatemala City. A gangster, he was used to surviving in the hopeless squalor of poverty. Just below his hovel was one of three spigots that supplied water for the forty-five thousand people who lived at a lower elevation than he. When the earth shook that night, the precipice of dirt and mud towering over his shack collapsed, sweeping him and his family into a hopeless darkness that threatened to extinguish their battered souls.

All the rhetoric about land reform had missed them. Hector needed to steal to eat. His mother walked miles each day on bare feet swollen by the filth of poverty, carrying on her head a basket of chickens to sell. Her hopes for a better life were faint when the earth shook. She would later recall thinking it was the end of the world and expecting Jesus to come and rescue her from her life of misery. Her worries were only for her wayward son and invalid daughter. Clutching them with withered hands, she waited out the thirty-five seconds that would determine their fate.

Dr. Coca Mazariegos lived high in the mountains. His clinic was open to all. He had been the target of the communists because he was a native Mayen, and also because he was educated, he wielded considerable influence through medicine, and he had married an American missionary. He was living proof that there is hope for the multitudes, and it does not come from the type of armed mob that held us in the Aceh police station.

Those who would control the multitudes do so through false hopes and force. Threats and bitter words are their weapons. Hatred pours out of their hearts. Usually they are people who have suffered some personal affront at the hands of those they now hate enough to kill. Couching their hatred in lofty rhetoric, claiming some sort of divine mandate or just cause, they incite the multitudes to take action by intimidating or annihilating those whose message of hope is true.

The multitudes have to decide which offer is theirs. They have to find a point of connectedness to the one offering them true hope. Jesus healed the sick, cleansed the lepers, and multiplied the loaves and fishes; and great multitudes followed Him. He gained enough influence that He had to be killed, or else those who controlled "public security" would lose their positions. He won the affections of the people by meeting their most basic needs.

It is the decision of the multitudes that will determine the outcome of the nation. China's Mao Zedong preached a common hatred of the landowning class. The people rose up, the landowners either fled or were killed, and the land became barren and unfruitful. The thought of a farmers' uprising became the fear that led to the construction of the Great Wall. Just a few years ago, when farmers began to gather at train stations in support of the students in the Tiananmen Square uprising, the army had to be called in to restore order. The message of hatred toward those in power had been so effective that even the new power-brokers—the ones who had taught the people such hatred—were themselves in danger.

Now the same hatred was being preached in Guatemala. In this Catholic nation, the multitudes were hearing a theology of social and political activism from French and Spanish priests come to stir them up against fellow Catholics with financial power and political clout. The Guerrilla Army of the Poor, funded by overseas interests and armed by weapons delivered during night flights from Cuba, were training in the mountains near the home of Dr. Coca Mazariegos.

Youth by the hundreds were being offered money to kidnap and kill executives and landholders. Private armies were assembling, and every Mercedes or BMW that drove through town was in the escort of a multi-passenger vehicle whose darkened windows prevented onlookers any glimpse of the armory contained within. Recruiters exerted strong pressure on these youth. They would be the masses seen in demonstrations with strategically positioned student leaders in their midst, ready to turn up the agitation at a signal from the leaders. They had been recruited and trained.

And then, the earth shook.

Having green eyes—being a landowner—was going to be a problem. The remote village where Don Lacho lay was a weapons storage facility for the Guerrilla Army of the Poor. The Mayen family had been landowners there for generations. Soon they would be forced to leave their lands in the peasant uprising planned for 1976. By midyear, the unrest would build to the point of overflowing in the capital, and youth from the city would come through the Motagua Valley to resupply.

Sympathizers in the small villages were ready to receive and supply those who would create constant unrest in the areas around the north and east of the city, until the government fell and the land would become theirs. Green eyes meant that you were of the landowner's class and would need to be suppressed by the multitudes. Nothing personal; they would just circle your house and ask you to come out to meet a hopeless future. If you did not, they would throw rocks and bottles and light fires until you paid them the proper respect. It was the same in China, the same in Vietnam, the same in Warsaw, the same in Indonesia.

And then the earth shook.

When the dust cleared on February 4, 1976, the hopes of the revolutionaries had been destroyed. Who would rebuild this nation? What possible hope could frustrated fanatics provide in the face of real human suffering? What words would explain how Don Lacho, Hector Zetino, and Dr. Coca Mazariegos had been shaken and spared? How do you mobilize a mob to surround a nation and cry out that an earthquake is partial in its destruction?

Natural phenomena create multitudes, and on that cool morning, a sad nation gathered its dead and began to mourn. For a time, things seemed hopeless. Then, help began to flow in from the northern nation they had been learning to despise. By noon, a reconstruction effort was mobilized by two men—a Canadian and an American—who had been sent to Guatemala months prior. How had they known?

Army hospitals were set up, and medicines were flown into remote areas by missionary pilots, while men like Dr. Coca Mazariegos worked for days to help the injured. Youth from the ghettos were mobilized by local churches to move piles of rubble, in hopes of rescuing thousands hanging from a timeline of dehydration and blood loss. One such group dug Don Lacho out of his house and helped the dazed old man to find shelter.

Thousands of people came from other nations to help meet the needs of these unfortunate people whose world was suddenly shaken. Without any political agenda, millions of dollars flowed into the ravaged country. Hope came on love's wings.

We were invited to rebuild a village where one hundred and fifty families had been rained down upon by their tile roofs. Just a few miles from the epicenter, the earth had been split, severing pipes that supplied water and thereby eliminating the only source of potable water for the population. One morning, after the American and Canadian asked our team to serve the needs of El Fiscal, we stood on a low ridge overlooking the devastation. The medics had been through it already. We could see the multitude looking up to us in search of hope. We accepted the task and, with prayer, launched an adventure that brought three men—Lacho, Hector, and Coca—together to create hope where hope was lost.

Our first task was to register people: Mayen, green eyes; Reyes, brown eyes; Rios, green eyes; and so forth. Before a week was out, we knew the racial divisions of this small population. We were most fortunate that our forms left no opportunity to register political or church affiliation. The earthquake had been impartial, and so were we.

Juan Reyes was the mayor. He presented a list of one hundred fifty families who needed temporary shelter, water, food, and clothing. Upon close examination of the list, Hector found that it was composed entirely of youths who had been recruited for Lacho's village. They were of similar ages, and in the rubble of their homes, we found materials designed to incite this mob to violence against their neighbor. When we asked the mayor about it, he shrugged his shoulders and said that a foreigner would never understand.

We suggested that he put his personal wars on hold until we had rebuilt his town, and we decided to put him in our "intensive true hope information program." He responded to love. He got honest about the needs of the people, and the town was rebuilt, complete with clinic, school, churches, and a beautiful water system. But greater still was the rebuilding of the relationships between the populations. Families were able to reconcile, and the instigators of hatred were asked to leave, as the multitude made a connection with peace. Caches of weapons were returned to the government, and amnesty was given to the youth. The President of the Republic extended a "Bullets for Beans" campaign, and most of the militia members in that region surrendered their arms.

Coca had a harder time of it in the mountains. The region had become a stronghold for insurgents. Training facilities were concealed behind the façades of schools, and farms had become factories for the production of heroin and cocaine, which were used to pay for the weapons needed to overthrow the government. As a medical doctor, Coca closed one eye to all of this and treated the local people without partiality. This practice kept him and his family safe, until one of the leaders of the insurgents decided that, to overcome the love that was being demonstrated, he needed to pour more hatred into the multitude. They couldn't stand the fact that the people were gaining real hope for a future that did not depend on killing their neighbors.

Coca received multiple death threats. He sent his family to the United States but remained in the mountains to serve the suffering. He treated army soldiers and local and foreign militants without partiality, until a night visitor informed him that he had to leave the nation in three days or be killed. The visitor pleaded with him to go, and he finally agreed, hoping to one day be able to return to his homeland.

I was asked to drive Coca, and whatever belongings we could stuff into a Volkswagen bus, to the safety of the United States. I was not worried about Mexico; my greatest concern was the first fifty miles, as a van filled with equipment, medicine, a Guatemalan doc, and an American driver would make a great catch for any young gunman. With prayer, I flew to Guatemala City to meet Coca.

Our plan was to leave the city at 6 p.m., which would put us in his village at midnight. We would spend two hours loading the van and then leave the village, heading north. If we went through the mountains instead of taking the coastal road, we would be in the vicinity of people he knew and had treated, so we could stop, if necessary. Of course, I never planned to stop at any home, because that could mean a death warrant for its occupants. It was clear that Coca had never driven a VW bus through the mountains, but it sounded like a good idea at the time.

We left on schedule, and although the tension was palpable, we made it to his village and loaded the van without incident. With a prayer and some tears, we headed north out of the village on the mountain road. With every blind curve and switchback, we expected to be stopped by a falling tree or a squad of gunmen.

By two in the morning, we had reached the main highway, a two-lane ribbon of asphalt winding its way between volcano peaks. Tourists love to ride the colorful chicken buses that move along slowly, taking all day to travel from village to village. But we were not there for the scenery. The road was in bad shape because of the earthquake, but the bus was new and amazingly powerful, for a late-seventies-model VW.

We passed Coca's birth village at dawn, and he openly wondered if he would ever get back there. We had kissed his mother, father, and little sister good-bye in the capital. There had been a great deal of emotion as their son, the hope of their futures, was forced from his homeland and practice. Pausing before the cathedral, we said good-bye to the town, then rejoined the northward road that would take us to Mexico and then the US.

I first saw the pickup truck in my right side mirror. It was swerving from lane to lane with each curve. Fear gripped my heart. I hoped it was just a drunk farmer on his way home. We came to a place where the road straightened out, and I got a good look at it just before heading into the next bend. It was a white Ford, perhaps a 1973 model, and it had wooden rails on the back—the kind one might use to haul cattle. This morning, the cargo was a group of weapon-wielding youth. Their rifle barrels were pointed into the air, but there was no doubt of their intent. Accelerating into the coming curve, I warned Coca that something was about to happen.

We took the curve to the inside, and as I straightened out for the bottom, I saw the trap ahead that was designed to capture us. There was an old Mercedes on the right side of the road and a multi-passenger car blocking the left lane. A man stood there, palm raised, expecting me to stop behind the Mercedes.

"Coca, get down on the floor," I shouted, and pushed him down. He knelt there, praying for the Lord to get us through this.

Slowing as if to stop, and making eye contact with the man on the road, I noticed that the other driver was also out of his car. Terror is so accustomed to having its way that it sometimes fails to account for the few of us who really do not care if we die, because we have a greater hope. The threat of death is effective only if our hope is found solely in this life.

"Stay down," I said, as I calmly slowed and looked in the mirror to see if the chase truck had caught up to me. I have no idea why, but it was not there.

Fixing my gaze on the eyes of the man standing on my side of the car, I downshifted, let out the clutch, and accelerated through the situation. We just cleared the Mercedes, and then, going about fifty miles per hour, the gears caught with ease, and we sped on toward Mexico. The next three hours were a study in hope. We expected gunfire at every curve, until we finally reached the international zone. Exhilarated by hope realized, we drove straight through Mexico and into the US, until we reached the northern state in which Coca rejoined his family and restarted his life.

The earthquake shaped those three lives and millions more. It broke the back of the beast of Communism. The youth have grown with education. And, while there still is crime, there are no more truckloads of militant youth searching to kidnap innocents and hold them for ransom. To be sure, there is political activity, but now the nation enjoys the peaceful transfer of power, as all parties work together for the good of the multitude.

〜

As we sat in our cell in Indonesia, I thought about the fear I had experienced that day. The threats, the mobs, the violence—it all came back as I heard again the sound of the hate-filled mob outside our barred windows. The Banker held up six fingers, and I settled in to think some more.

# FOURTEEN

# A BRIGHT, SUNNY DAY

I t was a bright, sunny day in Ulan Bator, Mongolia. We had been on the train for five days when it finally stopped. Anyone who says it is a small world has never ridden the rails from Hong Kong to London. It is *not* a small world.

Our group of five was tired of train travel. Eager to stretch our legs, we asked the conductor what time the train would leave. He responded in German, saying "Fier," and holding up four fingers. Released for a few hours, we quickly grabbed some of our belongings and strode across the platform into the sleepy town of Ulan Bator. Capital of what was then called the Soviet Republic of Mongolia, this 1985 whistle-stop town had once been the crossroads of two great cultures.

We walked through streets, nearly empty of people. The buildings were primitive compared to the splendors of Beijing. We had passed the corral areas of the nomadic herds and a junkyard filled with rusting Russian military hardware. Now we wanted to get some fresh bread, maybe meat of some kind, and make it back to the train in time for our journey to Siberia.

At each shop, we were greeted with such warmth that we forgot to keep track of time. Handshake by handshake, we made new friends. The Mongolian people were very receptive to our attempts at communication. We found steaming bread and cakes and were having a great time. We went from building to building, shaking hands with the people and having our picture taken with them. From a glance at a watch, we calculated that we had about half an hour before we had to be back at the train.

After a few more handshakes, we walked quickly back to the platform. There was no train in sight. None. An entire international train had disappeared. I approached a guard and asked, using supplemental hand gestures, "Where is the train?"

He replied, also using hand gestures, "Gone."

With my hands, I asked, "Gone?"

"Da," he said.

I held out my hands like a criminal acquiescing to be handcuffed, and said, "Take us away."

Laughing, he took us to the train station, then went off to find someone who could speak English. After the requisite round of clarifying, placing blame, and apologizing, we settled into the adventure and waited to see what would happen next.

Two of us were loaded into a car and taken downtown. There, we were questioned by a matronly Mongolian woman who turned out to be someone important. She explained that we had returned late for the train, but not to worry; they had advised the Russians, and our things would be removed from the train when it reached the border. Now, as to ongoing arrangements, she wanted to know if we had any money. We had little between us, because we had left everything on the train, including our passports and other travel documents. Each of us was literally without a name or country. She promised that she would take good care of us.

We were taken back to the train station and allowed to rest in a room with no door handle on the inside. It was very clean and neat, and we were comfortable. We spoke little but were not unhappy; at no time did we feel at risk.

At about six in the evening, we were ushered to a train. It was another of the steam engine type that we had ridden to this point, and as we entered our compartment under police guard, the other passengers took quick note of our "foreign" look. They were instructed to give us lots of space, and they obligingly closed their compartment doors.

Now we began to speak to each other concerning the dilemma we would face in the morning. Our bags were sure to be searched, and they contained valuable Bibles and cassette tapes in Mongolian and Russian. Transport of these items in the quantities we carried could mean only one thing: We were smuggling them across the Soviet border. We were headed into a certain international situation. As team leader, it was my job to figure this out.

I was really hungry. The bread we had bought was gone, and I had to think, which is always easier with food. I tried to find a dining car but was told there was none. It seemed that everyone on the train was in uniform. We found out through a student who spoke some English that this was a military train of troops returning from the war in Afghanistan. With that news, I decided to stay in the compartment.

I mentioned before that one member of our team had a disorder requiring him to eat every six hours; otherwise, he got really grumpy. I chose the corridor rather than the complaining. Standing alone at a window, I reflected on our situation. We were on a Russian military train approaching the Siberian border. Ahead of us, the police certainly had our passports, our money, and enough evidence to put us in jail. We did not have food or water, and the night was going to be tense, considering the attitudes in the group. Things did not look good.

"Deutsch?"

The question startled me.

"Nyet Deutsch," I responded without thinking. "Amerikanski."

"Amerikanski!" the voice roared back.

The hand was big enough to cover both of my shoulders. I looked up and to my left, into the smiling face of the largest man I had ever seen. In one move, he swept me down the hall and into his compartment. There, five other men in uniform were enjoying black bread and fatback sandwiches with brown mustard and vodka. The sight brought back wonderful childhood memories. When times were very bad, we would take a strip of pork fat, put it on wheat bread, and spread the warmth of hot mustard over it. Filled with the energy my family and I needed in the freezing winters, I think there could have been no better meal to ward off the cold Gobi night. They were Russian military, celebrating going home.

"Amerikanski," he announced, as they made a place for me to sit. He ducked back out into the corridor and soon returned with the rest of our group. To their offer of vodka, I informed them of our Christian faith, and they respectfully changed to black tea.

The train sped through the night as we shared about our lives. We talked of Cuba—two of the men had been there as technicians—and of the war in Afghanistan. I was embarrassed to realize I was unaware of this struggle. We talked about missiles and nuclear weapons. We talked about our countries being enemies. We were frank and cordial. They said they had always wanted to tell Americans how they felt about things. They also wanted to hear how Americans felt about Russia.

We began to exchange songs. They sang military and folk songs, and we sang worship songs. As we alternated, we tried to learn each other's language. We were thrilled to see them sing "hallelujah" and raise their hands, as we had. The night was filled with love for each other. We, who were cast in the role of enemies, would, for one night, be friends in the common bond of food and song shared.

Our host gave the word, and we were returned to our cabin. With stomachs full and hearts overflowing, we settled in for a deep sleep. The enemy had become our friend, and we had hope for the morning.

Dawn brought us to the platform on the Mongolian side of the border. We were ushered from the train to certain trouble. We watched for our singing companions, but they were nowhere to be seen. There, in the police department of the train station, were our things. Each bag had been emptied and inventoried. The currency was laid out, one bill at a time, and the serial numbers of each bill recorded. The tapes and Bibles had also been inventoried and were arranged in neat piles. The chief, another matronly woman, asked us to verify all of the contents and sign for them. We thanked her for her thorough care of us, and she allowed us to repack our belongings while she stepped into her office. Upon completing the packing, we were invited to have tea with her, at which time she asked me to sign a letter, along with its English translation. I signed both and returned them to her.

The letter verified that we had been well treated and that all of our possessions had been returned, with nothing missing. She was emphatic in stating that we were guests in her country. She could not vouch for the Russians, she said, but Mongolia was a friend of the United States.

We were amazed and delighted at her attitude, and, with thanks, we took on the challenge of getting all of our stuff into Russia. Customs was a breeze, as was immigration. We were greeted with friendly smiles everywhere. These people were supposed to be our enemies. Every one of us had been raised with the association of having to run to a bomb shelter when the ballistic missiles of Mongolia and Russia arrived with their deadly payload. For being enemies, these people were extremely friendly.

⌒

As I sat in this cell, thinking about the youth in the street, I remembered that big Russian officer. He had been trained to wage warfare against us. I had been trained for warfare against him. He had grown up thinking that I would bomb him and his family in order to become richer. I had been raised to think that he would "nuke" me and my family to take over the world. We had been made enemies by those who had taught us to be so.

What about these young people? Who was teaching them? Jesus said to love our enemies, but today, we never get the chance to meet them. As the day wore on, I decided that, given the opportunity to meet some of these people, I would at least be friendly about it.

Maybe Leck was right. Maybe it was an honor in the sight of the Lord to show forgiveness in the face of persecution. Why did I think of them as the enemy? Who had first said they were my enemies? Where had I gotten that idea?

My reverie was once again interrupted. Interpol was back.

# PART IV:

*"I send you…."*
—Matthew 10:16

Now the names of the twelve apostles are these: first, Simon, who is called Peter, and Andrew his brother; James the son of Zebedee, and John his brother; Philip and Bartholomew; Thomas and Matthew the tax collector; James the son of Alphaeus, and Lebbaeus, whose surname was Thaddaeus; Simon the Canaanite, and Judas Iscariot, who also betrayed Him.
—Matthew 10:2–4

Are they Hebrews? So am I. Are they Israelites? So am I. Are they the seed of Abraham? So am I. Are they ministers of Christ?; I speak as a fool; I am more: in labors more abundant, in stripes above measure, in prisons more frequently, in deaths often. From the Jews five times I received forty stripes minus one. Three times I was beaten with rods; once I was stoned; three times I was shipwrecked; a night and a day I have been in the deep; in journeys often, in perils of waters, in perils of robbers, in perils of my own countrymen, in perils of the Gentiles, in perils in the city, in perils in the wilderness, in perils in the sea, in perils among false brethren; in weariness and toil, in sleeplessness often, in hunger and thirst, in fastings often, in cold and nakedness; besides the other things, what comes upon me daily: my deep concern for all the churches. Who is weak, and I am not weak? Who is made to stumble, and I do not burn with indignation?
—2 Corinthians 11:22–29

# FIFTEEN

# THE HINDU KUSH

**M**r. Mark."

He was very professional.

"We are now satisfied that you had no idea what was happening here today. We see that you happened to be in the wrong place at the wrong time. This is an innocent mistake. We are sorry for the difficulty you are having, and are talking with the leaders of the group to allow you to leave. Please be assured that we are doing everything we can to ensure your safety."

I had no idea why an Interpol policeman was at a sleepy little town; why a Muslim radical was stuffed into an "I Love America" T-shirt; why a helicopter had been sent for tourists; or why anyone would bring a surface-to-air weapon to a religious rally. I also had no idea why a "Ninja" was negotiating for peace or why a squad of commandos was on its way to the scene. But it looked pretty interesting from where I sat.

Until that day, I had thought the Chinese held the record for making things appear other than they were. This group was pressing to steal that title. With more questions than answers, and time passing without direct pressure, I sat back to recall other pressure-packed days from my life.

⌒

A few years prior, we had decided to cross the Hindu Kush, that passage between Pakistan and Afghanistan that is so contested today. We assembled our team in Singapore and flew to Islamabad. From there, we purchased bus tickets for a drive that would take us over the 17,000-foot pass and into China. It was the same route Marco Polo had taken, one of the ancient silk roads. We were carrying several thousand copies the gospel of Luke and the book of Acts, translated into the Uyghur language—the tongue of the Arabic people thought by some to be one of the lost tribes of Israel, by others to be a displaced people group. They inhabit the desert strip of oil-rich land between China and the Muslim nations.

The ascent was wonderful, the Indus River providing a spectacular opportunity to ride the cable boxes that are the only link to many mountain villages. Passing K-2 and glacier flows, we saw many things I never dreamed existed.

We ate the same style of noodles and pizza that inspired Polo to take the recipes back to Italy. The team was fun, and everyone was getting along fine, even with the altitude sickness and travel stress. Finally, we crossed the peak and began winding our way down through sand dunes and rock faces to the border crossing at the Chinese city of Tashkurgan.

It was there that we ran into a difficulty. Ambition had conquered reason, and my son and I stood with fifteen bags at our feet, while the tour group had moved on through customs. No one takes fifteen bags for a bus trip through the desert. Of course, the customs officials wanted to know what was in the bags; and, of course, when they found the books, they wanted to conduct an in-depth interview. After dispatching the rest of the group to a hotel in a neighboring town, they invited my son Sammy and me to a private interview.

We were escorted to a modern office building where we were introduced to the Chief of Customs. He allowed us to rest in the hallway while he and his team made a thorough inventory of the contents of our bags—a process that took about two hours. A sparrow flew into the hall while we were there. It flitted from side to side, and in and out through the window. Though captive, it was free. Though free, it was captive. I watched him for some time, thinking of the old hymn "His Eye Is on the Sparrow."

The Customs Chief returned from the search and inventory and invited us into his office. A Uyghur national, as opposed to a Han Chinese, he was very interested in why we had brought the "Jesus" films and books in his language rather than Chinese.

"Some friends asked us to carry them, since we were coming this way," I offered.

The answer was completely true. I had no idea of a delivery plan or contacts or any such thing. It was not my plan, and they were not my books.

He thanked us for our interest in his people, the Uyghur. We were then released to the Chinese police, who were pleasant and obliging after being confronted with the fact that they had separated me from my son, something they were not supposed to do unless I was officially arrested and charged. They brushed the complaint aside and turned us over to the Chinese Border Police, who recorded our information and then took us to rejoin the group.

We learned that each of the group members had been questioned individually, and that my other son, Matt, was the only one to have been given a real shakedown. He was frightened, and I could see that all of our efforts over the years of making the Chinese our "friends" and not our "enemies" were going to perish if something positive did not occur soon.

The following day, we traveled to the ancient city of Kashgar. What a place to see. From the ancient mosque to the horse market at the bazaar, ancient cultures of East and West blended in a display of color and tradition. We spent an enjoyable day walking and praying for the people. The head imam of the mosque received us warmly and asked if we had brought the New Testament. He had been listening to Far East Broadcasting and wanted desperately to have a New Testament. We were delighted to give him one before pushing on.

The next morning dawned with a knock at the door, followed by the phase we love to hate: "Mr. Mark, could you come with us, please."

As we walked down the hall to the questioning room, I kept telling myself, *I love these guys. They are just doing their job. There is nothing personal about this. They are nice people.*

Sam called out from behind me, "If they throw us out, we are flying. We do not want to leave by bus or train."

"Mr. Mark, I have to inform you that you are under arrest. The nature of the charge against you is a threat to the national security of the People's Republic of China. This is a very serious offense. The punishment can be very serious.

Please cooperate with us fully and give honest answers to our questions." He was serious.

The room was like a movie set: the single wooden chair beneath a lightbulb; the two policemen blowing cigarette smoke in my face; the "nice guy" trying to "help" me through the situation as he rifled through my personal effects. Together, these three men were difficult to love; they were rapidly becoming enemies.

They had identified my Bible and passport as the two items that would affect me most. The English speaker started taking papers from my Bible and asking me about each one. They were bulletins from past services at various churches, a photo of a child we were trying to pray off of drugs, and the like. I watched the way he handled the Book. There was no respect given to the Word of God. I was not personally offended, but I tucked the thought away for use as a preaching point in future messages.

For now, I dwelled on Jesus' message to His disciples in Mark 13:11: "*When they arrest you and deliver you up, do not worry beforehand, or premeditate what you will speak. But whatever is given you in that hour, speak that; for it is not you who speak, but the Holy Spirit.*"

I relaxed, ready to watch the scene play out.

"You are in big trouble," the officer said. "A threat to national security is like an espionage charge. I would suggest you tell us exactly why you have come here." His sincerity was mind-boggling.

"I am a threat to your national security?" I was equally sincere. "Would you please tell me how a middle-aged fat man who does not even speak Chinese can be a threat to the national security of the world's largest nation?"

It was a good question, and I enjoyed asking it.

"You are a Christian, right?" he asked.

"Of course I am," I responded. "Everyone should be."

"That is a threat to our national security," he explained, as if I should understand.

I was dumbfounded. "How is my personal faith a threat to your national security?" I asked honestly.

He smiled. "Everywhere you go, you will tell people about Jesus, right?"

"Of course," I answered. "Sharing our faith is like breathing for a Christian."

"That is a threat to our national security."

He nodded to the other two, as though seeking affirmation. They nodded.

"How is that a threat to your national security?" I asked.

"If they hear, they will believe."

He leaned forward, and our eyes met. I looked for some sense of light in this man's eyes. He was quoting what Paul had written in Romans 10:13–17, a passage which compels many Christians to become missionaries. I saw no light in his eyes.

"If they believe, we cannot control them," he added.

He was very serious now. We were nose to nose.

"You people will not be able to do in China what you did in Europe!"

His emphatic declaration sparked my next question.

"What did 'we people' do in Europe?" I was sincerely eager to hear his point of view, however rehearsed it probably was.

"Communism will not fall in China! You Christians will not take us over. You are a threat to our national security."

He began thumbing roughly through the pages of my Bible for effect. I thought he would throw it at me, but he regained control and sat down again.

"Please give me my Bible," I said respectfully.

"Oh, you want this book?" He held it out of reach, taunting me. "What is so special about this book?"

Now he had done it. You might as well ask Jonas Salk what's so special about the polio vaccine. Ask Bill Gates what's so special about computer software. Ask NASA what's so special about space travel.

"Let me tell you, son," I said. "That is the last thing I touch before I sleep. It is the first thing I reach for when I wake up. It is the Book that changed my life. It is the Book that saved me from hell. It is mine, and I will ask you to give it to me."

Eyes locked, hearts aflame, we faced each other.

He shrugged and handed me the Book.

The next morning, our group was escorted to the police station, where we were fingerprinted and documented; our passports were updated with an earlier-than-planned departure date. Afterward, we traveled by bus and train for more than a week, with police escort. They were concerned about whom we would see and what we would say. In every hotel in which we stayed, they briefed the staff concerning us.

And still we had daily opportunities to share the hope that was in us. The briefings with the hotel personnel served to arouse their hunger for hope. They wanted to know about a faith so precious that we were ready to risk everything for it.

When we boarded the flight in Xian to depart from China, a policeman came on board, and the flight attendants asked us all to produce our documents for him. From my seat in row 17, I called out, "Are you looking for Mr. Mark?"

He affirmed that he was, then motioned for me to come forward. I did. After a close inspection of my passport, he bid me a safe journey and then exited the plane. I turned around in the aisle and faced a plane full of nervous people. I decided to explain.

"You are probably asking yourselves, 'What did he do?' I am guilty of preaching Christ in China. This is the state of Christianity in China. The believer here is seen as a threat to national security because he has found hope in Jesus. For this message, we are being asked to leave China today. It is our joy to fly with you all."

The passengers applauded as I returned to my seat, and for the duration of the trip, we enjoyed the best in-flight service we have ever received.

A year later, I was in Long Island, New York, to participate in a missions conference. One of the speakers worked in that region of China and asked if he could talk with me. In the presence of only one of the pastors, he said to me, "Sorry if they gave you a rough time last year."

"What?" I asked, surprised that he knew about it.

"Yes, it was all arranged. We felt that you would have the maturity to pull it off. The bags that were confiscated were delivered in the region. Thank you very much."

⌒

Who is the enemy? It wasn't this brother, and it wasn't the police. It wasn't the kids in the Aceh heat, and it wasn't even the Irate Imam. The enemy is the one who tries to keep people from knowing the truth that will set them free. (See John 8:32.)

Through the demonstration of love and patience, we have seen the worst situations turned around for good. The banker held up six fingers. As the tension level escalated, I gained strength from what we have come to call "The China Experience."

# SIXTEEN

# THEY WERE BACK

The Ninja, the Interpol, and the Uniform stood at our doorway, about to give us the hourly update. As the afternoon had worn on, it had become clear that negotiation was not going to win the day; at some point, a real show of force was going to be required. How that would play out was up to them. Our role was that of the sincerely sorry lot who happened to be in the wrong place at the wrong time.

Four hours had passed since the Irate Imam had shouted through the window. Several events had occurred since then. The mob had fallen into a pattern of attacking the building four times an hour. They had succeeded in burning our car and the police chief's car. They had gained entrance to the building twice, had broken out the windows, and had set fires in the front offices. They had rejected all offers of negotiation, wanting only for us to be handed over to them.

A question rolled around my mind: *Why didn't they just point the surface-to-air missiles at us and blow off the front of the building?* I decided not to voice my inquiry._When I looked over at the Banker again, he held up seven fingers. I felt a bit nervous. The Doctor's vein was raised again, and the Chinese man had that look one assumes when he is about to take on the whole mob single-handedly. It was a good time for the leadership style of quiet confidence, made possible by the presence of the Lord and the memory of His solid track record of displays of His grace. It is true that today's pressures prepare us for future victories.

According to the report of our three friends, it was going to be dark soon. That was bad news, unless the commandos made it there before nightfall. The three felt there was no way they could defend such a small building at night, so, when the army arrived, there would be a lot of shouting and shooting, and we should stay low and be ready to do whatever we were told.

Looking beyond them, I saw the open arms locker and the orange-taped banana clips being issued to the police. They looked tired and nervous. Some of them glanced at me with disdain, others with indifference. I shall forever appreciate the professionalism of the Indonesian police.

*Sit tight. Stay away from windows. Do not try to escape on your own. Help is coming. We will get out of here.* Rounds were fired in the front, and away they went to their stations of duty.

I looked at the Banker. His smile was not reassuring, and his eighth finger was up.

Whose plan had this been? It was a fair question; and, had a team member asked it, I would have taken the responsibility, to prevent any division in this time of pressure. Thank God the men on our team were mature enough to not ask it aloud, even though we could see the same question in one another's eyes: *Are we here in the will of God?*

Returning to my seat, I pondered the conflicting doctrines: the one that says if you are in the will of God, everything is wonderful and goes well; and the other, which says if you are in the will of God, you will suffer in this life. (See, for example, John 16:33.)

Then came the real question: *Did somebody else get you into this, or did you do it yourself?*

Four events in my life have brought me face-to-face with this question, Who sent you here? It is most often asked by someone who decides that I do not have the cunning, the intellect, or the spiritual power to be in the place I am. Or, in the case of the Interpol, someone who wonders how could I be so uninformed and stupid.

⌒

One morning, the phone rang in my small office in Pennsylvania. My secretary said that Lester Sumrall was on the line. Dr. Sumrall has long been a hero of mine. As the founder and president of the Lester Sumrall Evangelistic Association (LeSEA), he was a pathfinder for those of us who desire to take the gospel message of healing and deliverance to the nations. I was shocked that he had called me.

"Are you Brother Geppert?" His voice, rough from preaching, commanded respect.

"Yes, sir, I am." I hoped I didn't sound too young to him.

"I hope I didn't interrupt anything important?" He was polite and powerful.

"No, sir. Glad to take the call." Actually, *thrilled* would have been a better word.

"May I ask you a few questions?" He was very polite.

"Sure, anything."

I was very interested to know how he had heard about me and what he wanted.

For the next fifteen to twenty minutes, he asked me questions about the people I had met and the places I had been. He had heard of my arrests, of the nations I had touched, and of my involvement with television in Pittsburgh. He knew that we took Bibles to other nations, beginning with countries in Latin America. I never found out how he knew. He was used to asking the questions.

He made arrangements for my wife and me to visit the LeSEA Broadcasting TV studios in South Bend, Indiana. We stayed at a lovely hotel, enjoying breakfast and lunch before our return to Pittsburgh. In everything, Dr. Sumrall was a gentlemen and an example of a supportive older minister guiding the younger man.

He and his wife invited us to a time of prayer, during which they placed their hands over our heads and commissioned us to answer the calling the Lord had placed on our lives. I understand that Dr. Sumrall had been commissioned in the same way by Smith Wigglesworth, who had received his own commissioning by George Müller. The memory of this experience has often given me strength, such as in Aceh.

The inevitable question we face in the apostolic ministry, as "sent ones," is "Who sent you?"

Unlike Robert Duvall's character in the film *The Apostle*, we cannot lay hands on ourselves. We cannot be self-motivated and expect to properly represent the Lord among the nations. But there is no doubt that there is, in the body of Christ, a place for those who carry on the mission of the "sent ones."

This was Dr. Sumrall's question, and it would surely be that of the Interpol and the Indonesian police once our situation ended.

"Who sent you?" is the question that takes the disciple out of the realm of self-motivation, dutiful service, and expected activity;—the realm of "What do you do?"—and into the realm of "Whose authority is behind you?"

Like the young teacher in Nepal or the Guatemalan who finds his self-worth, the disciple will often receive a picture of truth and run with it as fast as he can. He will preach till he drops, pray till heaven answers, give till he starves, and then look for more to do. This level of commitment was demonstrated by the apostle Peter when he said, *"Lord, not my feet only, but also my hands and my head!"* (John 13:9).

When Jesus was sending Peter off to feed His sheep, He corrected this mind-set with these words:

*When you were younger, you girded yourself and walked where you wished; but when you are old, you will stretch out your hands, and another will gird you and carry you where you do not wish.* (John 21:18)

This Scripture captures the essence of the ministry of those "sent ones." Toward the end of the disciple phase of maturity, they realize the truth of what a man named Dr. Costa Deir once told me: "Your life is not your own. First, you belong to Jesus; He bought you. Then, you belong to your family; they love you. Then, you belong to the church; they sustain you. Then, you belong to the nations; they wait for you."

Those in the ministry as "sent ones" preserve these four close relationships. They will die for Christ. For them, *"to live is Christ, and to die is gain"* (Philippians 1:21). It was this thought that gave us hope, no matter what the outcome of Aceh would be.

"Sent ones" love their families; a study of their children will find them heading corporations, leading in the health and education professions, stable in marriage, and guiding the coming generations.

"Sent ones" are sustained by the church; they do not have time to sustain themselves financially. The symbiotic relationship they have with the local church releases spiritual, human, and material resources for the benefit of both.

The nations truly wait for them—the police in every land want to experience authority without corruption. True authority is ordained by God to serve those who walk in His ways. In a later chapter, you will hear about a man who waited a lifetime to meet someone who had been raised in a Christian home.

Dr. Sumrall and Dr. Deir were more than familiar with the admonition to let no one call you an "apostle." They held to the better phrase of "sent one." And they both were fully conversant in the principles involved.

Being a "sent one" is simple: A nation has a need. You are made aware of that need. A church receives an offering for that need. You deliver the offering to the point of need. As you travel, you become aware of the opportunities to demonstrate the love of Jesus by meeting others' needs. You report back to the church on other opportunities to meet needs and to glorify God in the process. The church prays about it, and when the Lord confirms the need, as well as His desire to meet it, He leads the church to contact you, and they send you out to meet the need.

The ministry of a "sent one" is extremely simple compared to that of a pastor. A pastor has to look after the flock, know their names, and minister to their needs; whereas a "sent one" just goes out and demonstrates the love of Jesus to anyone who is waiting for him. Granted, there are dangers of being a "sent one," such as when those who wait are an angry mob in the street. But that is just part of being a "sent one."

Many people want to know how a "sent one" differs from an evangelist. The "sent one" is a rock on which the church can be built. He has the ability to meet physical needs by organizing, administering, and delivering supplies and aid. The evangelist can proclaim the message with sign and wonders, achieve breakthrough in difficult places, and visibly demonstrate the power of God to work miracles. The "sent one" can do all of these things and also leave an indigenous structure behind—a rock on which God can build His church. (See Matthew 16:18.)

⌐

Such are the things on which a "sent one" reflects as the sun sets on his life for what may be the last time: *Have I run the race? Have I fought the fight? Have I completed my "course"?*

As I sat there in Aceh, the resounding answer in my spirit was, *Yes, you can come home now.*

The peace that touched my soul in that moment was like nothing I have ever felt before or since. I was ready to meet Jesus face-to-face. The feeling grew as I walked about the small space. It was a peaceful, light sensation. I looked in the faces of my friends and thought I saw a bit of it there, also. Beyond human resolve, it was the promised preparation of the Holy Spirit.

# SEVENTEEN

# THE CALL

Ivana Madzur had taken the step. She was being sent to Berlin. She loved the Lord. She loved her mother and father. At my last dinner with them, we celebrated the wonderful young woman who was their daughter. Her church was sending her. They affirmed her call and her gifts; though she was young in age, she was not short on experience. They were excited to send her.

A nation was calling. In fact, many nations were calling. The whole world was calling for relief for the lie of atheism. People living behind the Iron Curtain and the Bamboo Curtain alike knew there was a God and that the state was not it. Their cry had reached her heart, and God had called her to respond. She was not the only one of their fellowship who hungered for the deliverance of the nations. Her priest, Father Roman Trzciński, cried out night and day for the deliverance of Poland.

Our meeting was a classic case of "Who sent you?"

Leaving the J bus at route's end, we found her waiting for us. It was late afternoon and we were about to meet the young man selected to restore spirituality to the Solidarity movement. Jerzy Popiełuszko, the spiritual father of Solidarity, had been martyred the year before. His body, having been wrapped with chains and dumped into the Warsaw River, had floated to the surface and been found by farmers several kilometers south of Warsaw. The Solidarity movement had turned political under the leadership of Lech Wałęsa, and the church was concerned about the secular slant it was taking.

The pro-Solidarity bishops met to select a replacement for Jerzy Popiełuszko, and they decided on a bright, well-respected young man involved with the youth movement, a charismatic man whose heart beat with those of the rising generation. The movement had a martyr; what it needed was another "sent one."

We entered the vine-covered prayer grotto, and there, far ahead, stood a solitary figure in European cassock. Robed in black from head to foot, his stance authoritative, he was the embodiment of what the Russians feared.

As we came closer, Ivana could hardly contain herself. "I know it is the will of God for you two to meet," she proclaimed, wringing her hands in delight. "I just know it is supposed to happen."

Father Roman greeted us with enthusiasm. Looking deeply into my eyes, he said, "You are the one."

Taken aback, I asked Ivana, "What does he mean, 'I am the one'?"

Not needing the translator, he said, "You are the one I have seen."

Their community had been fasting and praying for a messenger to come, sent by the Lord, to answer a very difficult question for the young people. As Catholics, they had only celibate priests and nuns as examples of full-time service to God, and they wanted to know if they could marry, have families, and still serve God. If this was feasible, they would continue in Solidarity. If not, they had some serious reservations about how far they were willing to continue in the movement.

"You are the one I saw in the dream." Father Roman verified every feature, from my eyes to my Levis. "You are the sent one."

We talked that night about another visit, one that would last twenty-three days, during which I would be accompanied by a charismatic Catholic priest, who would affirm to them the message I would bring. I was sure Father Mike Salvagna would come. He loved the Lord, was filled with the Holy Spirit, and would certainly be sent by his community. We planned more than fifty meetings with the youth, as well as a final Eucharist with the bishop of the home church of Pope John Paul II. Little did we know at the time that the Lord had even more in store for us. We sang through the night, and I listened to their stories of life under the Russians.

These atheist Communists couched their natural hatred of the Poles in political and spiritual phrases. When cornered on the economy, they persecuted the church. When their state-run factories failed to meet their production quotas, they made life more difficult on the Poles. The state police were brutal, and the church often had to meet in the forests to avoid detection. Ivana was one of those the Lord had raised up, and the visitors who rode the rails were a veritable lifeline, bringing materials. The church needed a prayer curriculum—something simple yet biblical. I suggested *Change the World School of Prayer* by Dick Eastman, and they asked me to bring Dick with me when I returned. Knowing that Dick is a "sent one," it was not difficult to comply.

With hugs all around, we set the time for the following spring and asked the Lord to bring it to pass.

I returned to the States to make arrangements. Mike was easy; he would be sent out by his community, as I had thought. We had to clear a schedule for Dick, but his ministry agreed to send him, combining the stop in Poland with a trip he had scheduled to Romania. With the plans settled, I headed back to China and the Trans-Siberian Railroad.

This trip went very well, and I arrived in Kiev to the blossoming of the tulips. Spring is beautiful on the Dnieper River, and the city was in full bloom. I visited the tomb of St. Andrew, another "sent one," who had come from Jerusalem after Pentecost and had brought the good news of Jesus to those in this valley and beyond. Spending a day of prayer in his burial place renewed my sense of the irresistible force of the multitude now traveling the world proclaiming the hope they had found in Jesus.

While I was sitting in the cathedral, a tour group was ushered inside. The guide sat down next to me and decided to try out some English. "Do you like the relics?" he asked.

"Yes," I replied. "Do you know who this man was?"

"He was some early Christian during that era," he said. "We no longer believe in such things. But the building is nice, and the architecture unique to the former period." He looked at me as if begging for a rebuttal.

"Not everyone has stopped believing," I said gently. "There are some yellow tulips among the red."

"But there were not many," he answered. Then, with a wry smile, he returned to his group.

I had no money in Kiev, yet another counterpoint to the impression that "everything goes easy when you are in the will of God" and a confirmation that "those who serve shall suffer need." In fact, I had been penniless for every part of the trip, as the two brothers who had accompanied me through China and Russia had needed all of their money to get to London. Dick and Mike would bring me some money from the church that had sent us, so it would be just a couple of days until I was eating regular meals again.

I spent all of the next morning in prayer. At noon, there was a power surge, silencing the habitual chimes and playing of the song of the revolution in Kiev. I felt the Lord telling me to board a train and get out of town. I stopped at the travel desk in the hotel to ask if I could leave that night. They were happy to accommodate me, and within an hour, I was on a train for Poland.

The train was packed with young people, some of whom shared their bread and cheese with me. With my stomach full, I slept to the rhythm of the rails and prepared my thoughts for the three weeks I was about to spend in Poland. Little did I know that the next morning's events would change the world.

We were delayed crossing into Poland. Not a problem; I watched an interesting television special on nuclear safety and wondered at the Russians' openness about their nuclear energy program. All along the railway, we had passed nuclear reactors and power plants. It was reassuring to see so much TV time given to safety. Especially touching were the scenes featuring children playing in the shadows of the cooling towers. Perfectly safe, perfectly clean, they were the pride of Soviet achievement.

Upon arriving in Poland, I made my way to Mr. Szymanski's house to await Dick Eastman's arrival. We would meet at the Forum Hotel, and then I would take him out to the convent. He did not arrive the first day, so I went on out and checked in with the Sisters of Saint Felix. They were happy to have someone to take care of, and I really did not mind the attention. These charismatic nuns were filled with such joy. Their worship was Holy Spirit filled, and their service was without equal.

The next morning, Ivana came to the motherhouse, and we all sat down to a big breakfast. I was ready for it and could hardly wait until after the time of meditation and special prayers. Father Roman was there, and Dick and Mike were expected to arrive any moment, having been delayed by one day. Mother Superior came in and joined us, carrying a tray with some kind of juice.

"Ivana," I said, "what is that?"

"That is iodine," Ivana answered. "Mother says we have to drink it."

"Why am I going to drink iodine?" I asked.

"It's for your thyroid."

"What is wrong with my thyroid?"

"Shh. Just drink it." She was emphatic.

I sought help from my friend Father Roman. "Do I have to drink this iodine?"

"You have not heard the news?" He turned and looked me straight in the face. "While you were praying in Kiev, a nuclear reactor at Chernobyl exploded. We are in the middle of a cloud of radiation that can kill if it gets into your thyroid, so we have been encouraged to drink the iodine to neutralize any effect of the radiation. It is up to you if you want to take it or not."

I sat there, putting together the pieces of the puzzle. I recalled the power surge, the urgency in my spirit to leave town, and the manner of prayer in which I was involved just prior to the surge. I thought of the danger we all were in. Dick and Mike were being sent into the cloud. It was all swirling around in a kaleidoscope of colors. I poured the iodine on a houseplant, finished breakfast, and headed for the forum to meet Dick.

He had brought with him several magazines and newspapers from the free world. He told me of the visions and dreams people had shared with him concerning his trip. He had almost called it off, but he said he knew that I was in the cloud, and that Mike was being sent to join us, and he felt that he had to follow through with it.

Dick Eastman and Mike Salvagna will always be in my heart as brothers who hazarded their lives for me and for the gospel.

⌒

Three others were hazarding their lives. The Doctor, the Banker, and our Chinese friend could be within minutes of meeting eternity. I looked across the darkening space and marveled at them. They were just ordinary people—they had no claim to greatness—but they had followed the Lord. They had been sent by Him to this time and place.

I am sure the apostles did not look the way they are depicted in the paintings found in grand cathedrals. In fact, if you research their ethnicity, you will find that they were pretty common people. They had grown from hope to belief, from belief to discipline, and from discipline to "being sent." Having proven their faithfulness and having been filled with the Holy Spirit, they were compelled to go.

Dick and Mike in Poland, and the three men with whom I had shared that afternoon of adventure in Aceh, had something in common with the apostle Andrew: They went where they were sent.

The peace was there again, and with it came the certainty that I would be seeing Jesus soon.

# EIGHTEEN

# WHO HAD SENT THEM?

W ho had sent them? Who had sent all these people trekking over mountains, riding the rails, walking through cities, eating pizza in the old towns of Europe's cities, and risking their lives in international incidents? Who had sent them? Was it a big organization? Had a church sent them as missionaries? Did they have a special sense of calling? A dream? An angelic visitation?

How did they know they were supposed to make one of these "faith journeys"? How did they manage to get time off from work? How did their families react? How often did they go? If they got into trouble, who would take care of them? Were they all young, or were some of them elderly? Did they go alone, or were they always in a group?

Who sent them? Who paid for their travel? How did they know where they would stay or what they would do? Who decided what they would eat or where they would sleep? Were these "once in a lifetime" events, or did they occur on a regular schedule? How much did each trip cost? How often did they go?

Who sent them? How were they trained? Did they all come from the same city? How was the itinerary decided?

As dusk slowly sapped the features from their faces, I looked about our sanctuary and studied my three friends. The Chinese man had been the first with the idea. It had come about in conversations we had about Islam—its spread and the significant places where Jesus would have us pray. Firmly persuaded that the whole global issue was the depleting resource of oil and the increasing demand of urban growth, together, we felt that Muslim forces were trying to control its field and flow, supply and demand.

Our interest was not economic but spiritual. We noticed a pattern over a period of twelve years: economic pressure, followed by population increase due to the Islamic practice of a man having as many as four wives and many children, followed by overcrowding and limited land resources, followed by the redistribution of property, including the allocation of tribal lands to urban dwellers in what *National Geographic* magazine had heralded as a great accomplishment of the Suharto, Javanese, government. We had been to Western, Southern, Central and Eastern Sumatra, but we had not gone north to Aceh province, the last to join the Republic of Indonesia.

Home to the ExxonMobil refinery, Aceh was strategic to oil flow. Aceh was considered 100 percent Muslim, and it was reported that Christians had a most difficult time there. The voices that arose from recently discovered mass graves gave evidence of mutual intense hatred. The "Java government" and the "Free Aceh" forces used the ideological struggle to fuel their uniformed, or rag tag bands, against each other. While oil was the issue, their passions of faith fueled the flames. "Free Aceh" wanted to fulfill their reputation as 100 percent Islamic. The Jakarta government, located on the island of Java, was sworn to uphold "Pancasila," or the "one god, many paths" policy, which is an abomination to monotheistic Muslims.

The Chinese man had heard of the plight of Christians in Aceh and had asked me if we could take a drive through the region, praying in significant places, to see if the reports were true. We had hoped to present our findings to various prayer ministries, to invoke their focused intercession. We were interested only in the spiritual side, being neither businessmen nor political activists. We had traveled through many countries in our endeavor to encourage people to pray for the nations, because we firmly believe that prayer is far more powerful than guns or money.

We talked about the plan many times throughout the following year. Checking our schedules, we found that mid-March looked good. We thought about who should join us, and we agreed to let the Lord send people to us rather than recruit them; we wanted His team, not ours. So, each time we found ourselves with a group of people who were inclined to pray, we mentioned the trip and then waited to see whom the Lord would send.

Nearly one hundred people had expressed a personal interest in coming on this trip. I laughed to myself as I thought of it. The cell in which we were secreted would not accommodate anywhere near one hundred people. How would the outcome have differed if they had all been sent?

Some could not clear their calendars for an entire month, which was the duration we projected for the trip. So, we gave them the option of joining us for as long as they were able, and divided the trip into different segments. Those who enjoyed scuba diving could meet up with us at the "Grand Canyon" of Aceh, an underwater festival of marine life. Others could join us for the "Cross Sumatra" trek, which would take them from one side of this mountain in the sea to the other. Others could join us for the "Encourage the Christians" portion, in which we planned to identify Christian churches in Aceh and stand with them in solidarity. Others could join for the "Future Development of Aceh" portion, which involved meeting with local leaders and identifying humanitarian ways in which to develop the region's access to education, medicine, and microeconomics.

We tried to make the trip possible for as diverse a group as we could. Yet, at the end of nine months, only two of the original one hundred were still interested: the Doctor—a trusted personal friend and veteran of trips to Latin America and Asia—and the Banker, who wanted to spend a month in daily discipleship as he worked to identify his mission for the second half of his life in Christ.

The three of us agreed to meet in Singapore. Each of us had the backing of our family and our pastor, as well as the necessary financial support. We convened; spent a few days getting accustomed to the time zone, the climate, and each other; and then made our way across the Strait of Malacca. Once in Indonesia, we hired a driver in Medan and headed north by car. We spent a great deal of our time looking at schools, clinics, and small businesses, developing a plan for microeconomic development based on our belief that the profits of the oil industry would not trickle down to the farmer and small business owner.

We four in our little cell had been sent by thousands of people who shared our common faith and understood the importance of acting out that faith by meeting human needs. We were not alone in our trial. We were not at all alone in that place. Because we had followed proper steps, there were people in Indonesia who knew of our whereabouts. There were people in Singapore, and in every other nation of Asia, who were tracking our daily progress. The Doctor had a network of people he kept up-to-date, as did the Banker; and I had 1,500 people praying daily for our trip.

Our families were definitely aware of where we were and what we were doing every day. The Doctor's wife and children, the Banker's wife and children, and my own wife and sons were very much with us in spirit as we awaited the outcome of these events. But even more present with us was the Holy Spirit.

Jesus is the One who sends us. He touches our hearts with a need. He continues to draw us to that need. He plants an idea in our minds concerning that need. He makes a pathway for our feet to get us to that need. And He accompanies us to the location of that need. In the West, we think of sending someone as saying, "See you later." In the East, there is a different understanding. There, when someone says "We will send you," it means "We will go together." When Jesus said, "*I send you out as sheep in the midst of wolves*" (Matthew 10:16), He meant that He would be with us in the midst of the wolf pack. When He sent the disciples "*into all the world…[to] preach the gospel to every creature*" (Mark 16:15), with the aim of making "*disciples of all the nations*" (Matthew 28:19), He also said, "*Lo, I am with you always, even to the end of the age*" (Matthew 28:20).

As I sat in that cell with those fellow "sent ones," I was very aware of the calm peace of the Lord. As dusk gathered in corners of the cell, despair was driven away by a warm sense of the presence of God.

I thought we would die. In fact, I was fully persuaded of it. And, because of that peaceful presence, I was ready to see Jesus, face-to-face. I knew He would meet the needs of my family. I had confidence that He would watch over them. I was honestly looking forward to seeing Him.

# PART V:

*"Do not fear those who kill the body but cannot kill the soul."*
—Matthew 10:28

*And being assembled together with them, He commanded them not to depart from Jerusalem, but to wait for the Promise of the Father, "which,"*
*He said, "you have heard from Me; for John truly baptized with water, but you shall be baptized with the Holy Spirit not many days from now."*
*Therefore, when they had come together, they asked Him, saying, "Lord, will You at this time restore the kingdom to Israel?" And He said to them, "It is not for you to know times or seasons which the Father has put in His own authority. But you shall receive power when the Holy Spirit has come upon you; and you shall be witnesses to Me in Jerusalem, and in all Judea and Samaria, and to the end of the earth."*
—Acts 1:4–8

*Then I heard a loud voice saying in heaven, "Now salvation, and strength, and the kingdom of our God, and the power of His Christ have come, for the accuser of our brethren, who accused them before our God day and night, has been cast down. And they overcame him by the blood of the Lamb and by the word of their testimony, and they did not love their lives to the death. Therefore rejoice, O heavens, and you who dwell in them! Woe to the inhabitants of the earth and the sea! For the devil has come down to you, having great wrath, because he knows that he has a short time."*
—Revelation 12:10–12

# NINETEEN

## WHERE HAD THIS CONFIDENCE COME FROM?

**W**as I crazy to try to imagine the ultimate escape—death—or was it a real confidence that allowed me to say, as Leck had high in the hills of Thailand, "Father, I ask You to forgive him, in Jesus' name"? I didn't know how it would come; whether we would be dragged into the street or shot in the cell and the building burned. I had no idea if we would be the hooded captives shown on TV and used to extort money from our families and home governments, or if we would just "disappear," as many trekkers do. But I had the confidence that, whatever our fate, I would see Jesus.

Looking about the cell, my eyes met the Banker's. He was relaxed, poised, and in deep thought. Each of us was. The crowd was growing louder, and we sensed the immanence of the final rush that would overthrow the police and bring them crashing into our cell, ready to send us to our eternal rest. The Banker held up nine fingers and offered a tense smile. Silence often says more than words ever could.

The Doctor looked at me. "I love my wife," he said. "I really love my wife. Oh God, forgive me; I really love my wife." Pressure level nine causes men to repent of every nasty word they have ever said to the ones they love. Suddenly, midlife crises are seen for the hopeless offers they extend.

The Chinese Man looked at each of us and, with typical Asian resolve, sat down to await the outcome.

The arrival of the Ninja, the Interpol, and the Uniformed Officer brought yet another situation update. The Officer spoke for the group.

"Okay, we have come to a serious time in this operation. The commandos are just a few minutes from arrival at the rear of the mob. They are expected, so there will be a battle there. They will quickly fight their way through to relieve us. We do not know which way the crowd will move. They may rush us. If they do, do not worry; we will protect you."

The Ninja picked it up from there. "We are going to close this metal door for your protection. Please do not open it for anyone. We are prepared for this. Please do not try to get out through any other way. Please remain calm."

After the door had closed, we took our positions for what we all thought would be the last few minutes of our lives. The Banker and I stood by the door. The Doctor and the Chinese Man sat behind us. The Banker broke the tense silence. "This is a number ten situation." For this man with 243 Golden Glove bouts and three martial arts black belts, we had reached the pinnacle of peril. It was quite an accomplishment for a doctor, a missionary, and a machinist, all of whom just wanted to travel and pray for some people. Taking a deep breath, we prepared to meet our Maker.

In the moments that followed, I thought of situations the Lord had allowed to occur that prepared me for this hour. They comforted me as I awaited the inevitable wave of the multitude-turned-mob on the shore of safety and order.

⌢

In the summer of 1978, I was walking door-to-door in the village of Zacualpa, located in the Guatemalan department of El Quiché. This municipality was the seat of government for twelve thousand people, mostly the El Quiché branch of the Mayen people. For reasons not yet fully known to anthropologists, these tribes left their jungle habitat at Tikal and fled to the mountains. I was there at the request of a development group, and my job was to determine whether the people would be receptive to medical, agricultural, and educational development. They were, and as a first step, I was going from house to house to give a Bible to anyone who could read Spanish. This was our way of sharing the good news of Jesus while also assessing the reading level, for guidance in developing educational projects there. On average, we found that one child in a family of as many as eight people could read. The rural schools were expensive, and in the Mayen concept of "family," each person has a responsibility to share whatever he or she learns with the rest of the family when they circle together in the evenings.

I was standing before an elaborate adobe structure at about ten in the morning, preparing to knock on the door, when a little boy took my arm and said, "Uncle, could you please follow me?"

He led me inside a hovel of straw a plastic roof and a dirt floor. There stood his mother, grandmother, and older and younger sisters. I began to share with him about the Bible and made the customary inquiries about his reading ability. Interrupting, he drew my attention to a man sleeping on a wooden door on the floor in the back corner of the hovel. He asked if I would pray for the man. I did, touching only the sleeve of his flannel shirt, not wanting to interrupt what appeared to be a deep repose. Having prayed, I turned back to the little group. We were just establishing the older sister's reading ability when the boy interrupted once again. He opened his mouth to speak, but no words came out. His eyes grew big as saucers, staring at something behind me. Thinking it was a spider, snake, or scorpion, I turned just in time to see the man on the door wake up, stretch, roll over, and go back to sleep.

Thinking little of it, I finished the Bible presentation and then continued toward my goal of identifying seventeen new readers for the day. The afternoon went well, until I was handed a note telling me to leave the town, or else be killed. I took it to the police to see if it was a legitimate threat, and they asked me to leave, saying that they could not protect me. This was the work of the Guerrilla Army of the Poor.

I left and spent the next six months working in another region of Guatemala. We had no computers or e-mail in those days, so I was not surprised to receive a hand-delivered telex. I was surprised, however, by the content. It was an invitation to go back and speak again in Zacualpa, where six pastors—one per month—had been killed in the time since I had left.

I checked with the authorities, and the police assured me that it was alright to go. I got a ride with a missions aviator and was met by a group of people who took me to the same adobe home. After a dinner of beans and rice, we were joined by a throng of people. The furniture was pushed aside, and people filled the room. Standing against the wall, I looked out through the window and saw hundreds of people surrounding the house. I asked my host about the meaning of all this.

"Do you see that man over there?" He indicated a gentleman across the room who appeared to be in his mid-thirties.

"Yes," I said, "what about him?"

"Do you remember him? He lived in a hovel behind my place. He had a small family. You went there and prayed for him."

"Oh, yes." Now I remembered. "I'm glad to see he is alright."

"You do not understand," my host continued. "He was dead. His body was lying there, waiting for the wake. These people have come to hear you because of this miracle. That is why the Army of the Poor had to get rid of you. The people were no longer afraid of them, because they felt you would also raise them from the dead."

I was amazed. I'd had no idea the man was dead. If I had known, I would have offered my condolences to the family and bid them a hasty farewell.

⌒

Standing now on the "safe side" of a metal door in the darkness of an unlit cell, I again felt the presence of the One who has the power over death. I could hear the sound of the battle outside and wondered how many would die that evening.

Looking at the Doctor, the Banker, and the Chinese Man, I wondered who would be the first to die. Would they just roll a grenade into the cell and kill us all? Probably not; the mass graves told the story of extreme butchery and savage torture.

These friends of mine were so peaceful. There was no panic, no argument, and no accusation. I could see that the confident peace and assurance of hope I felt was theirs, as well. We were ready to meet Jesus. All of us had a certain anticipation of the moment we would face Him, having died in His service.

Then I could hear the sounds of battle as the commando-driven mob began their rush on the building. The firefight was just reaching the interior hallway. There were sounds of gunfire and men calling to each other. I was too preoccupied to even consider moving from the door. The Banker was equally focused. Leaning forward, he was positioning himself for defense, should it suddenly spring open.

*Why did the stuffed T-shirt mention Ambon?* The question flew into my mind like one of the bullets careening through the hallway. Ambon had been lovely before the irate imams had inflamed the people against the Christians.

# TWENTY

# THE GEM

Ambon is the gem of the Maluku Islands, located about a thousand miles from the town where we were awaiting our destiny. Walking there had been a delight. The oil-rich area was home to docile people groups who spent their lives working for the development of the island paradise. At the request of a national Christian movement, I had traveled there to teach on prayer. My host was a former national director for A&W Root Beer, an American fast-food chain, and I thoroughly enjoyed the fellowship of their fledgling church.

Ambon was one of those places to which the Javanese government had sent denizens of their overcrowded cities. They had come from the southern tip of the island of Sumatra and were, for the most part, members of a radical Muslim group called the Madurese. Their native island of Madura was known as a place where seven Christian churches had been burned. I had been there and had interviewed the oldest Christian leader, who explained to me that a faith that permits a man to take four wives and encourages many children will eventually displace a faith that permits only one wife and suggests family planning. His church had grown in previous generations through large families.

His church building, and everything in it, had been burned to the ground two years earlier. He had complained to the government in Jakarta, and they had provided money to rebuild. However, the point had been made, and he and his followers knew that they could be taken to the church at any moment and burned alive, as others had been.

This same group, the Madurese, had shifted to Surabaya, a city ghetto teeming with malaria and dysentery, before relocating to the sweet breezes of Ambon. There, it was just a matter of time before their population would become dominant in the democratic process, and Sharia law—the moral and legal code of Islam—would begin to take over society.

Ambon was filled with teenagers. I watched the city's basketball team practice, reminded again of the ability of athletics to unify rather than divide. Pointed toward a common goal, these young men left their religion behind in favor of cooperation. I was impressed with the way they moved the ball. Their anticipation of each other's location on the court reflected the hours they had spent training together. The idea that an irate imam could ignite a fanatic frenzy that would pit one of these youth against another seemed beyond belief.

After practice, the team attended a youth rally, at which I spoke of Jesus' impartial love for everyone and of our need for impartial love for one another. They all responded to prayer, Christian and Muslim alike. These young people humbled themselves before God and asked that unity and love prevail in their community. There was not one hint of racial or religious tension in the place.

Ambon is known for two beautiful structures, the first of which is the Islamic mosque dating to the fourteenth century. Its emerald grandeur attracted me from the moment I arrived in town. When I visited the mosque, I sat for an hour or so and thought through the history of Islam in the islands that would one day become the Republic of Indonesia. Certainly, there had been "conversions" to Islam, but the strategy implemented in most cases had been to populate, propagate, and dominate. The same thing was happening in the US, in states like Michigan and New Jersey. This mosque, set on a hill on the eastern side of the city, had been a center for the domination of the region. Its minarets, fashioned of local hardwood, were beautiful and majestic. From their towering height, prayers were broadcast into the bustling valley below.

About two miles across the city was the second noteworthy structure in Ambon: the Dutch Reformed Cathedral. Equally grand, its white steeple raised high above the valley population, a statement of European colonialism.

The town rested in the peaceful relationship of these twin towers. The commercial center had been developed by the Chinese, who had come to the region in the fifteenth century. Their interest in the region was primarily economic; fittingly, the simple Chinese temple was dedicated to the god of prosperity. Politically, they were interested in peace above all else. In typical Chinese fashion, they lived austere lives while amassing fortune for future generations. Five avenues of shops offered everything from stereos to steam engines. This blend of Arab, Chinese, European, and local cultures had worked in unity to create an absolutely beautiful example of how good life can be.

Then it happened. Police reports are inconclusive as to who ignited the fire that burned the commercial center to the ground and sent thousands of local youth to their graves. Some say it was over an offense in a relationship between a Muslim boy and a Christian girl. Others say that the population had reached an exact balance of Muslim and non-Muslim, and that the non-Muslims had started the fight in an attempt to drive out the Madurese settlers.

Others said it was "outsiders," sent to disrupt the harmony of the place. Whatever the combination of logs thrown on the fire, the heat was intense. In one eyewitness report I heard, a group of children on a Sunday-school outing were suddenly surrounded by a mob of Muslim youth led by a man in his forties. One of the children, a seven-year-old boy, was held by the larger boys and told to deny Christ and declare the Prophet. When he refused, a machete took off his right arm. Again he was told to reject Christ and declare the Prophet. Again he refused, and the machete cut off his left leg below the knee. Caught up in the frenzy of mutilation, the youth allowed the other children to flee into the forest, while they continued to decimate the boy. The horror-stricken children ran to their homes and reported the incident to their parents, who took to the street, enraged.

Months passed. Thousands died in the bloodshed. When dispatched troops failed to cool the violence, they became the targets of both Muslim and Christian mobs. The battles raged night and day. The Christians defended the cathedral; the Muslims defended the mosque; the storefronts of Chinese merchants were burned and looted, their owners having fled the region. At the last, the twin towers stood over a field of bloodshed and destruction.

When the dust settled, there was only one place that had not been buried in the rubble of ruin. In the center of what had been a beautiful city—the pride of the islands, the gemstone of the wedding ring of the Indonesian marriage of peoples—was the basketball court. There was no sound of teammate calling to teammate. There was no team. They had been persuaded to become the exact opposite of the thing they had dreamed of becoming. Fueled by rhetoric, their anger ignited by adults, the youth had turned against each other.

⌣

What had the stuffed T-shirt meant with his declaration, "This is not Ambon"? And why had his friend stood there in silent distress when he had spewed forth the words, "This is my friend; he is a Christian"? Why had the tone not matched the words? Why had the face of the "Christian" not reflected the faith? Why had he spoken not a word?

Things were heating up again outside the metal door. We could hear the sounds of fighting in the building, and we realized it would be only moments before someone prevailed. From the cheering of the crowd, we felt that things were not going our way. Blinded by the rusting panel before us, and not at all certain of its protective power, I watched the Banker prepare for battle. He flexed his hands and made certain his footing.

How would they do it, this frenzied mob? Would they try to get one of us to deny our faith for their amusement? Would they take us to some jungle camp and keep us there for years, until our families presumed us dead? Would they use us as pawns in a negotiation with Jakarta for the release of their brothers held prisoner there?

I knew that the US government would not negotiate. Our ministry would not negotiate. We had no money to pay, nor would we ask any of our donors to put up the money. These people would ask for millions, or for political concessions; but they would never secure either of those things. I hoped they would just throw open the door and kill us all with a burst of automatic weapons fire. I fully expected to watch it happen as our spirits left our bodies for our heavenly home.

The persuasions of life and death wrestled in my mind. On the one hand, I would suffer death in this cell. On the other hand, I would see Jesus face-to-face. At what point would the Holy Spirit lift me from the situation? How much pain would I feel? Could the Lord arrange a quick exit from this life, or would He need a testimony to be spoken? How much grace could be drawn from the future hope that was in us? How real was our salvation?

Jesus had endured the cross, looking forward to the hope that lay before Him. Would we have three hours, three days, three weeks, or three years? What would our lot be? All of these questions raced through my adrenaline-charged mind. The Banker was cool, set for action, poised.

# TWENTY-ONE

## WHAT ULTIMATELY CONTROLS A MOB OF PEOPLE?

What is it that ultimately brings an unruly mob under control? Is it the satisfaction of the thirst for blood that follows the sacrifice of an individual? Is it the arrival of a uniformed mob whose strength is perceived to be greater? In Ambon, the uniforms became a focal point of common hatred. I supposed that their deaths caused at least some of the poisoned passions to abate.

What would it take for several thousand fanatics to drop their drives of passion and hatred and walk away from four Christian testimonies waiting to be offered? In some cases, they like to play cat and mouse, offering peace and then striking the unassuming individual. Would they tie us in a row and march us through town as trophies, a declaration of their superior manhood over the governments of Java and the United States?

There was no seven-year-old boy here. Would they strike down the one they perceived to be the weakest, emotionally, and mutilate him before the others? Would they show preference to the Chinese Man, not wanting to arouse the ire of a neighboring government? I determined that when the door finally opened, I would step in front of the others. It wasn't gallantry; I really felt the presence of the Lord equipping me to take the hit. It is a rule in our groups that the leader takes the hit, whether it is arrest or physical abuse; we do not stand back or run from a situation.

Clothed in robes of righteousness, I was ready to see the Lord. Very quickly I recalled the twenty-five years I had spent in ministry with Him. I thought of my salvation experience, of my Christian heritage, and of the faith of my parents and those with whom they fellowshipped. If the Lord had determined that I was ready to be offered at the age of fifty-one, then so be it.

In those moments, I thought of a martyr who had gone before me. He had been a family man with three little children. His nation of Laos was caught in the dawning reality of the decline of communism and the emergence of a capitalistic, free-market economy. The residual hatred of the United States for its use of chemicals during the Vietnam War had scarred people to the extent that they hated anything associated with America.

This man's receiving and preaching of the gospel of Jesus Christ had landed him in a Laotian jail. During his term, his wife fell ill during flu season and passed away, leaving their children without a guardian. When the government received word, they agreed to release the man, on the condition that he "sign out"—that is, sign a document saying that his conversion had been coerced and that he had not understood what he was doing.

On the appointed day, he signed out and was released from prison. His children came to collect him, and the four of them walked happily together through the jail yard to the gate, which was opened for them. As they started down the street, a man approached them, produced a pistol, and began to shoot the father. The final, lethal round was shot at close range. The oldest child, a daughter, attempted to shield her father's head with her hand; yet the man shot right through her hand, killing her father. That is terrorism. That is a statement meant to be communicated to others, just as I am now communicating it to you. That is the price people pay every day around the world for the crime of saying, "I believe Jesus Christ is the Son of God."

What price would we pay that Aceh day?

The shooting stopped. The Banker and I were face-to-face, each of us with a shoulder to the door. We could smell the gun smoke; we could hear moans in the hallway. We looked at each other and awaited our fate.

There was a knock. A voice said, "Open the door."

Remembering the Ninja's instructions, and with the Banker's agreement, I slid open the metal slot. My eyes met those of the man on the other side of the door. Was he my executioner or my deliverer? Was he the one sent of God to dispatch me from the affairs of this life, or was he the one who would throw a hood over my head, beat me for a while, and then drag me as a trophy out to the waiting mob?

"Open the door." His order was enforced with the large automatic weapon in his grip.

We looked to the others for agreement, then stepped back and opened the door.

He stood and looked at us. The weapon was hot and heavy in his hand as he lowered the barrel toward us. His face was streaked with sweat and dirt; his eyes were filled with the horrors of combat. He stared at me and said, "Are you Mr. Mark?"

"Yes," I answered, focusing on the gun barrel.

"Are you a Christian?"

Ah, the question that can take you to heaven. I was ready to go. Beyond fear, beyond thoughts of torture, resigned to whatever fate the Lord had in store for me, and bolstered by the ever-increasing sense of the presence of a loving God, I said, "Yes, I am."

I was ready to go. All issues resolved. Peace in my heart. Absent of fear. I was ready to see Jesus. I had heard His voice. I had felt His hand upon me. I had walked with Him among the nations. I had seen Him raise the dead. I had known His great comfort. Now I was going to see Him face-to-face and say, "Thank You." I was ready. He was there, just as He had promised He would be.

"Catholic or Protestant?" The question was out of the picture.

What a crazy question to ask a man who is ready to see Jesus. *Who cares?* I wanted to say. *Just do whatever you have been sent here to do, and let's get it over with.* I could see myself joining Peter, James, John, and the others who had given their lives for Christ. I was ready for the front row in heaven. I was prepared by the Holy Spirit to enter into my eternal reward, dispatched from the earth by this young gunman. What a crazy question to ask a man who is ready to go.

"Protestant," I answered, as I felt the hope leaving and the reality settling in.

"So am I," he said. "Stay here. We have some cleaning up to do, and then someone will come for you. Get down and crawl along the hall. It is dark. Take his hand, and he will lead you. There are many people here who want to kill you, so please stay down."

With that, he left. We got down and looked at each other. A quick smile was all we could manage; the tension of the moment had left each of us drained. Within a few moments, another man arrived. Following his instructions, we crawled through the hallway and clambered over the seats of a Travelall that had been backed up to the charred door of the jailhouse. An armed commando sat atop each of us and pressed us into the floorboards. They were polite, professional, and uncompromising in their demand that we keep our heads down.

I lifted my head briefly, to capture the moment in a memory that shall never pass. The building had been burned. Our car had been burned, and next to it was the police car that had suffered the same fate. A military truck was parked there, its windows smashed out and the metal showing the scars of attack. Another truck was parked in front of our vehicle, to obstruct the view of the mob.

They were on the other side of the street, The Ninja stood before them, a large automatic perched on his hip, and watched for anyone who would try to cross the road or throw anything.

Three more commandos approached our vehicle. One took the wheel, one assumed the front passenger seat, and another went to move the truck for our exit.

"Get on the floor, keep your heads down, and do not lift your heads up, no matter what happens." The orders came from the commando in the passenger seat.

He looked at me. "Are you Mr. Mark?"

"Yes," I answered.

"One of my men died for you today. He took a bullet through his eye—"

"Quiet!" barked the officer who was driving. "He is not to know."

Feeling devastated at this new awareness of just how desperate a situation we had come through, I settled down on the floorboards and thanked the Lord that I was alive.

Through the night we sped, four happy Christian men being swept through the warm, tropical evening in a military convoy. After about twenty minutes, we were allowed to sit up. For the first time, we could see the faces of those who had come to save us. They were very professional, with their eyes focused ahead of us; they did not say a word. With the passing of the miles, we began to realize that our situation was not over; it was merely changing location.

We arrived at a military base and were escorted to a large conference room. "The Lieutenant" was young. He introduced himself as our translator and presented a synopsis of our situation. We had walked into a tense political confrontation. The act of handing out Christian literature would be blamed for inciting the demonstration; but, in actual fact, something else was going on—something he was not authorized to explain. We were to wait here at this facility for our safety and for an investigation of the events.

Our passports had not been returned to us, so I asked if we were under arrest. He told me to think of it as "protective custody" and said that he would let me know if and what charges would be filed against us.

My three friends walked about, surveying the building in which we would be kept for the next few days. I sat in a soft chair and thanked the Lord for leaving me here on earth. I had been ready to go, but the thought of rejoining my wife and kids had suddenly become more important. The Lieutenant cautioned us about going outside or standing in front of the glass doors. The concern was that if our presence here was discovered, an even greater mob would gather and attack this post.

As the others stretched their legs, I sat with this young man. "What actually happened there?" I asked him.

"I cannot tell you," he answered. "Just pay attention to the types of questions they ask, and you will be able to figure it out."

"I understand you are a Christian." His eyes met mine.

"Yes, I am."

Saying those words didn't have the same feel as it had in the cell.

"So am I," he offered. "I was posted here because I am a believer. There are two of us in this unit. The other is the Commander. That will not help your situation, but, before this all begins, I want you to know that we are extremely proud of the four of you."

# TWENTY-TWO

# THE DAYS PASSED SLOWLY

T he days passed slowly. We slept on the tile floor of the conference room. We were constantly under guard. The air-conditioning was freezing, and we had to pay in US currency to use the toilet. We were taken for questioning at a moment's notice, day or night, by one of a variety of individuals, ranging from friendly to antagonistic.

My first session started at midnight immediately after our rescue. I followed the Lieutenant's suggestion and listened closely to the questions. At first, I was disarmed by the fact that the man asking the questions was the same fellow we had followed when crawling out of the cell. Plainclothes now, and accompanied by four or five scribes, he chain-smoked as he pressed into my space.

After confirming some basic information about me, all of which was readily available on my passport, and completely ignoring my questions concerning our arrest, he leaned in closer and shouted, "You are CIA!"

Amazed, I sat back in the chair, but the people behind me put their arms across the back of my chair and pressed me forward, into a cloud of his cigarette smoke.

"You are CIA," he insisted, "and I am going to prove it!"

He looked fierce, this deliverer-turned-accuser.

"What makes you think I am CIA?" I asked.

After the pressure we had been through, this situation struck me as almost comical. I have no idea what a CIA agent is like, but I am definitely not one, nor have I ever been. If, by "CIA," this man meant "Christian In Action," then of course; but I was not associated with any US government agency, and our foundation receives no money from any political entity.

"Yes," he shouted into my face, "you are CIA, and I am going to prove it."

"You had better stop chain-smoking," I replied, "or you are going to die the slow death of lung cancer, which will spread through your body and kill you."

Looking at his cigarette—his fifth of the night—he asked if I knew how he could quit. His departure from the CIA accusations was a relief. It seemed that his heart was not really in this interrogation session. I think that what he really wanted was to go to bed. It had been a long, strenuous day, and this young man needed some rest.

"What makes you think I am CIA?" I asked again.

"Your age, your haircut, your glasses, your watch, and the place where you were. And the fact that you are not afraid of me."

"Afraid of you?" I asked. "I was going to be killed, and you came and saved me. Why would I be afraid of you?"

"Look," he said, "you were in the wrong place at the wrong time. You all look well trained. You, especially, stay cool under pressure. The other one walks like a cat. The Chinese man has no nerves. And the other American talks nonstop. You look to us like a trained team."

It was then that I realized what had happened. The four of us had reverted to our previous military training. We had been prepared for what to do in the event of capture, and we had done it. Instead of acting like a group of missionaries who knew only how to kneel down and accept the inevitable, we had been attuned to the situation and the people involved, causing those with similar training to suspect us of being on a clandestine mission. My interrogator had noticed that I stared directly into his right eye when he talked to me, and interpreted it as a lack of fear. Meanwhile, I had simply slipped back into a practice I had been trained to do many years ago.

By 2 a.m., he'd had enough. Tired from an emotional day, he had me escorted back to the conference room. Once reunited, my companions and I gave thanks to the Lord for our safety, prayed for our families, and got a bit of sleep, in preparation for the next round of questions.

The process continued for the next three days. The police brought in a group of "teachers" and instructed us to cooperate fully with them by telling them every detail pertaining to who we were and why we were there. During the night, the Banker had managed to contact his wife. He had simply ripped the plastic cover from an office phone and made the call. She had notified their pastor, who had called the US Embassy in Jakarta to find our whereabouts.

We refused to give our interrogators any further information, insisting that the signed statement from us was all they needed. "Charge us with a crime, or let us go" was our unified position; beyond that, we boldly refused to cooperate.

They got the Commander to persuade me to change our course.

I explained to him that we were beginning to show signs of cracking, emotionally, under their method of questioning. We had nothing to hide. We were not lying to them or concealing anything from them. I asked him if we could please make this the last day of the process. Then they could evaluate our testimonies and do whatever they had to do to move us back to our homes. I pressed the point that we had broken no law in Indonesia. Any loss of property or life had been the result of the mob of Indonesians attacking their fellow countrymen. And, though we were sorry for any part we had played in the situation, we needed to move on.

He was happy that we would cooperate, and he gave me his word that he would do everything in his power to expedite the process. And so, we entered the last full day of questioning.

They put me in a room with the chain-smoker. Now, every time he went for a cigarette, I reached across the table and took it from him. He was trying to quit. I told him about the technique that had worked for me—I called the name of Jesus every time I wanted another cigarette. So, there he was, calling on the name of the Lord while he questioned me.

Next, we had a different interviewer—a distinguished gentleman in his sixties—who began in a friendly fashion. His English was quite good, and I basically liked him. The plan was for him to get a statement from me, and then to confirm or discount it by calling one of the others in and asking him the same key questions.

The man began by asking me to tell him about how I grew up—my education, my military service, what I did for a living, and why I had been in Aceh during those days.

I took him step-by-step through the process of being born into a Christian family, receiving a children's Bible as my first book, having perfect attendance at Sunday school, and doing morning and evening devotions with my family. I told him about the impact of David Wilkerson and Kathryn Kuhlman on my life. I told him about being a teen youth leader and about my years of rebellion before my faith had become my own.

He sat spellbound as I related to him the process of Christian growth—the significance of the Bible, prayer, and fellowship in forming young lives.

After a break for coffee and the bathroom, we returned to our walk on the road of testimony. Together, we traveled through my college years, my years of service in the military, my marriage to a Christian girl, my rededication to Christ, and my years in business.

We broke again for lunch—a first for us—and then we walked the path of God's call on my life to preach to the nations: my return to school for preparation, my early years in missions, the development of missions in a local church, the creation of a Bible school, the training of others to take the good news into the world, and the eventual founding of South East Asia Prayer Center (SEAPC). At no point did the group seem bored or antagonistic to my story. The former chain-smoker took notes on all that I said.

When other officers chimed in with a specific question about why we were there or where we had gotten the materials we had been giving out, the former chain-smoker brushed them aside. He seemed enthralled by my testimony.

Around three in the afternoon, we caught up with the present. I explained that we were a team of four: a foundation president, a doctor, a banker, and a local Chinese man, who served as our guide. We had come to Aceh to look for a potential platform from which SEAPC could become involved in humanitarian efforts there. Because we were taking photos of clinics, schools, farms, homes, and other personal property, we had desired to bring a gift to give to the people, to compensate for our intrusion. The books and cassettes had come from a friend of a friend, and, since freedom of religion was guaranteed by the constitution of the Republic of Indonesia, we felt free to give these as a "thank-you."

He was amazed at my testimony.

"Mark," he said, "I would like to thank you for sharing so openly with me. I am a Muslim, born in a Muslim family. I have never heard the step-by-step testimony of a Christian born in a Christian family. Now I understand so much more of the way you think and the faith you have.

"Aceh will be a free republic soon. Our representatives are in Geneva and will meet with your government. They have already agreed to recognize us as a country once these hostilities are over. When that happens, I will be a leader in the new Aceh. Would you then come back and help us to develop our nation? We need medicine, education, and economic development, and I would like to invite you to return."

"I would be delighted," I responded, realizing that this was little more than the customary Indonesian apology at the end of what could have been a distasteful exchange. "But, could I ask you a question?"

"Certainly. What would you like to know?" He sat relaxed, as did the others in the room.

"Why did you think we were CIA?"

The group seemed a bit taken back by my candor. They glanced furtively at each other before I had my answer.

"We were told that the action that would drive the Java government from Aceh was to begin that afternoon. When you four came to the police station, the people thought that you were a team of CIA agents sent to take out the station from within. They started the riot to cover for you. When the station was not taken, they then decided that you had broken your promise, and they took the situation into their own hands."

⌒

Was it disinformation? Was it the truth? Administrations have changed since that day. September 11 happened. ExxonMobil has negotiated a new deal with Aceh. Who knows for sure what actually went down on that afternoon in March 1999? Many times have I thought back through the events of that day. I have discussed it with my three companions, all of us comparing the questions we were asked. I saw the Banker once more, in China; I traveled again with the Chinese Man; and the Doctor and his wife have rekindled their marriage.

The next morning, we were photographed, fingerprinted, charged with being missionaries on tourist visas, arraigned, tried, convicted, handed over to the Immigration Police, escorted to the city of Medan, blacklisted from Indonesia, and put on a plane to Singapore. Even after all that, I have kept in contact with the Lieutenant.

Recently, *The Economist* ran an article about the Strait of Malacca and the flow of oil from the Persian Gulf to Japan, Taiwan, South Korea, and other markets. The writer referred to Aceh as the key to the whole plan. When I saw the article, I thought that you, the reader, might like to read this book. As events unfold in their step-by-step adventure to globalization, you should know about the "stuffed T-shirt," "the Ninja," the "Interpol," and a group of four who have seen it face-to-face.

Where does a person's faith fit into a globalized economy? Is this the new economic "deliverer" of the oppressed? Are we really to believe that the youthful multitude engaged in a dusty demonstration in Aceh is going to find hope for their futures in a free-trade agreement or a globalized economy? Is their hope to be based on a society without personal beliefs? If they are people of religious discipline, will they eventually be forced take up rockets, grenades, land mines, and missiles to protect and spread that belief?

And what if they become "sent ones"? Will that mean they must become Arab militia or mounted cavalry? Already men are "martyred" through suicide bombing. Are they heroes in the struggle for freedom from oppression, or are they pawns in the new surge toward uniting all under one banner?

# TWENTY-THREE

# THE TIMES HAVE CHANGED

The world is now feeling the impact of what was once experienced only by people in remote places such as Aceh and Ambon. Jihad, or holy war, has spread around the globe. In the aftermath of 9/11, places like Spain and Turkey have replaced Manhattan in the headlines. But what of the remote villages of people who live every day in fear of sudden attack? What of the multitudes who try to find hope in refugee camps, until it becomes clear that they have been forgotten by the world at large? What of the unfortunate women and children who happened to get themselves caught up in last night's precision bombing and now, in the clear light of day, no longer have health or home?

Most of us ignore the headlines of the latest bomb blasts and UN debates in our haste to see what the markets have done or where oil prices are going. We have become so desensitized that we view an Arab militia in the Sudan turning woman and children into widows and orphans as a "humanitarian crisis" rather than the genocide it really is. From Dearborn, Michigan, to Durban, South Africa, we have learned to say the right things and do the right things to keep from upsetting the latest global bully.

Jesus saw the multitude and called them *"sheep without a shepherd"* (Matthew 9:36 NIV; Mark 6:34 NIV). He promised to feed His flock and to carry

His lambs in His arms. To the Christian, He is the Lamb become Lion—the Prophet King. To the Muslim, He is the coming Judge of the world; He is a prophet to be obeyed.

To the Palestinian woman at the well, He said, "*Whoever drinks of the water that I shall give him will never thirst*" (John 4:14). She believed His words and went to the city which is now Nablus, telling others, and the whole city came out to believe in Him. (See John 4:30, 39.) Her actions resulted in eternal life for those who had been hoping something would happen to elevate them from their lowly status.

Among Jesus' disciples were fishermen and public servants. Even the Roman soldier given the task of His execution declared, "*Truly this Man was the Son of God!*" (Mark 15:39). Greeks, Romans, Jews, Arabs, Africans, and Asians have found love for former enemies by embracing the Son of Love, Jesus Christ. He is the One who has torn down the wall of partition so that, in Him, there is neither Jew nor Greek, Barbarian nor Scythian, male nor female, slave nor free; we are all one in Christ. (See Colossians 3:11; Galatians 3:28.) The bonds of love form multiethnic, multilingual teams of people who travel the earth, demonstrating the message of the Master through acts of kindness and self-sacrifice.

He sends them. They are not self-motivated. Often, they find themselves in places they would not naturally go. They are of different races and backgrounds but unified in a common faith, hope, and love. The people to whom they are sent see the love, find the hope, and come to the faith.

Some "sent ones" are not well-received. They are persecuted. Some of them die at the hands of those unwilling to relinquish control of the multitude.

Therein lay the conflict we found in Aceh. There was an agenda. Some other drama was being played out on the same stage. I have often wondered if a Travelall carrying three Westerners and a Chinese man arrived in town after we did, considered the situation, and continued north. I suppose I shall never know; but love won the day.

Now, as I sit in Tibet five years after the "Aceh incident," as it has come to be called, I wonder about a lot of things. The chain-smoker made the connection to the new hope. I have had contact with him. The last interrogator has also begun to follow the disciplines of Christ and is preparing to demonstrate His love through service to the people. The Lieutenant kept in touch with me for more than a year and was growing strong in grace when last we communicated.

The United States government has changed administrations and, in the process, has become embroiled in jihad. "Free Aceh" is still negotiating in exile in Geneva, and young people are still dying in paradise.

When I could not return to Indonesia, I headed north from there and found a wonderful open door in Tibet. Now, working as a guest of the government that thrice asked me to leave, I am working with a team to bring health care to children. A delay in government process has allowed me to write these things down for you. I hope you have been inspired by the stories of faith and love you have found on these pages.

Christian growth and experience are not a "once in a lifetime" proposition. They are a step-by-step process—from multitude to believer to disciple to "sent one" to martyr. As we follow in the footsteps of Jesus, we find Him to be the Giver of faith, the Giver of hope, and the Giver of love. The prices we pay pale in the glory we will see as we follow faithfully in His footsteps.

I hope our paths connect as a result of this book. There are so many widows and fatherless children in the earth, all of them desperate for hope. As different religions argue over oil rights and weapons of mass destruction, let us be examples of what James calls *"pure and undefiled religion"* (James 1:27). Let us bring hope to this multitude of millions who, herded by war, disease, and natural disasters, are truly *"sheep without a shepherd"* (Matthew 9:36 NIV; Mark 6:34 NIV).

# AFTERWORD

# STEPS TO BECOMING
# A "SENT ONE"

The sending of laymen into the mission field had been embraced by all denominations. We have facilitated short-term teams since 1976, enabling carpenters to rebuild ravaged villages, doctors to rebuild ravaged hearts, and loving, compassionate people of all walks of life to rebuild ravaged people. From farmer to physiologist, from tractor operator to teacher, people of all professions have discovered the rewards of serving those who are unable to help themselves. One of our more regular participants has often said, "These two weeks each year add value to the rest of my year. When I go to work in the morning, I know that some part of my work this day will help one of these who have such great needs."

The pathway to a meaningful "vacation with a purpose" is simple. It is easy to be sent. First, think about a group of people who have a need. You can conduct research online, through your local church, in *National Geographic* and other magazines, at universities, or through your employer, to name a few options. Many corporations have noticed a tremendous boost in employee morale after sponsoring a relief mission or training project in a developing region of their home country. It is not difficult to inform yourself of the opportunities available to you.

Next, you should contact the organization(s) working in the areas where you feel led to serve. The Banker and the Doctor had contacted me through mutual friends. We had not anticipated spending our day being defended from an irate imam and his band of unhappy people, but we certainly loved the local people and had the resources to be of help to them. Before contacting a specific group, think about it, pray about it, and ask for information; find out if they will put you in touch with someone who has participated in one of their previous trips or projects. Be sure to ask "Who pays?" during this step. Any answer other than "We do" means that you do.

Next, submit your idea to a trusted friend or your supervisor, as well as to your pastor and/or church leaders. Give them the opportunity to get involved in sending you. This gives you the emotional support necessary to overcome separation anxiety and allows them the opportunity to participate vicariously in your journey.

One of our more frequent travelers owns an auto repair shop and saves a percentage of every account in a special fund for his travels. He takes pictures on every trip and has them printed, filling photo albums he puts on display in the waiting room at his shop, so that his customers may see where some of their money is going. Many people choose his garage because they get to see a portion of the fee goes toward feeding the hungry children in Cambodia. He has many notes from clients who are thrilled to participate with him in his newfound sense of worth.

Years ago, the Melody Beauty Salon in Springdale, Pennsylvania, was a major sponsor for child relief in Latin America. The stylists there donated a part of every account toward finding and feeding kids. Certainly, there were a few clients who stopped patronizing the place, but the vast majority of their ever-increasing clientele were touched by the opportunity to help sponsor travelers who were meeting the needs of children overseas.

Habitat for Humanity has set new horizons for people who want to do more than give money to projects. Now you can travel a short distance and get hot and sweaty for a good reason. The backing of Oprah and President Carter has lifted this "good idea" to a tangible, and now global, demonstration of love. By sharing their personal heartfelt desire to help people, Habitat has mobilized thousands of volunteers. Sharing your idea with others is not self-exultant. Actually, it can be very humbling.

# PRAYER OF SALVATION

While reading *A Faith to Die For*, you have seen that there are five levels of spiritual growth. The reader progresses from the multitude to becoming a believer. From a believer, he grows in discipline until he becomes a disciple. The disciples were entrusted with specific tasks and sent out to accomplish them as "sent ones."

The blood of the martyrs is the seedbed of the church and the soil in which the Word of God can prosper and change nations. A martyr is one who gives his life for the cause of the One in whom he believes. This state of selfless willingness to die is made possible by the power of the Holy Spirit. Jesus promised that after the Holy Spirit had come upon us, we would receive the power to be martyrs for Him. (See Acts 1:8.) The martyr's faith becomes so life-consuming that he is ready to die for it.

Every great path begins with a first step. The first step in this world-changing path is to come out from among the multitude and make a personal decision to accept Jesus Christ as your Lord and Savior. Jesus is the only One who can transform our lives, taking us from the multitude to believing, disciplined, world-changing faith.

If you are ready to take this momentous step, please join with me in this simple prayer:

Jesus, I ask You to come into my life. I ask You to forgive my sins. I give my life to You.

When you said those words, believing in your heart, your name was written in heaven. Jesus will now become active in your life. Find a solid Christian and follow him or her. Get a Bible and read it daily. And please contact me at SEAPC@hotmail.com. I will help you find a Disciple Maker in your area.

God bless you,
Mark

# ABOUT THE AUTHOR

Mark Geppert is founder and president of the South East Asia Prayer Center (SEAPC). He has taught seminars on prayer walking, microeconomic kingdom business principles, and team building to leaders in Latin America, Asia, Australia, Africa, and Europe, as well as throughout the United States. He is known as a "master communicator" though his work in radio and television.

Mark has over thirty-five years of international experience in over thirty countries and has authored four books. His first, *The Attack Lambs,* has over fifty thousand copies in print and has been translated into ten languages. Mark is ordained through Elim Fellowship of Rochester, New York, has served on the staff of several churches in the United States, and has most recently established and pastored the English-speaking congregation of the Church of Singapore (Bukit Timah). He is currently teaching, networking, overseeing, and inspiring existing projects and new avenues for sustainability and evangelization.

# S E A P C
## South East Asia Prayer Center

In 1991, a small group of individuals who were led to pray for 10 Asian countries founded the South East Asia Prayer Center (SEAPC), a nonprofit prayer organization that has grown to include members from over 30 nations. These members are dedicated to helping others find fulfillment in Jesus through praying, training leaders, sharing the good news, and meeting the needs of children all around the world. The four main platforms of this ministry are:

+ Evangelism
+ Church Planting
+ Discipleship
+ Leadership Development

In order to carry out this fourfold mission, SEAPC sponsors projects to improve health, education, parenting, and microeconomic development in South East Asia. This global community sustains a child-sponsorship program, builds churches and schools, hosts Vacations with a Purpose, and much more.

### Get Involved

There are many ways to get involved with SEAPC:

1. Pray for them. SEAPC was built on prayer and continues through prayer.

2. Financially support one of many projects, such as sponsoring a child, building a church or school, participating in the Vacations with a Purpose, or leading a local Mobile Prayer Team.

3. Become an advocate for those who are touched by SEAPC. Connect with members through the Web site, newsletter, online blog, or other SEAPC communication tools.

### Contact SEAPC Global Community

Phone: 412.826.9063
E-mail: info@seapc.us ♦ Web site: www.seapc.org
Address: P.O. Box 127, Oakmont, PA 15139